Just Speak Up

Olga Geissler

Compass Publishing

3

Just Speak Up 3

Olga Geissler

© 2009 Compass Publishing

Acquisitions Editor: Casey Malarcher
Content Editor: Garrett Byrne
Copy Editor: Vino Murugesan
Cover/Interior Design: Design Plus

Email: info@compasspub.com
http://www.compasspub.com

ISBN: 978-1-59966-418-7

13 12 11 10 9 8 7 6 5
15 14 13 12

Contents

How to Teach This Book

The best way to teach speaking is to have students practice speaking. This book has been developed to introduce a wide variety of speaking topics to students. Each unit also presents a number of activities to scaffold speaking tasks for lower-level or less secure speakers. However, it is not mandatory for higher-level and more advanced speakers to work systematically through all of the activities. Because the speaking topics are related by theme rather than specific content, the material in each unit is flexible and adaptable.

The lesson plan presented here is suggested for a class that requires significant support for each speaking task. Classes that do not require as much support may be able to jump right into the topics and start talking. It is left up to individual instructors to gauge how thoroughly each step of this lesson plan needs to be implemented in their classes.

Suggested Lesson Plan (60 min.)

Step 1

Activity 1 (10 min.)

Warm-up with Listening

Have students look at the unit topic. Ask the class to brainstorm a few possible questions they might ask someone about the topic and write them on the board. While students are suggesting questions, take time to briefly discuss how students might plan an answer for a few of the questions. For example, point out which questions should be answered with examples of personal experiences and which should be answered with opinions.

After a reasonable list of questions is written on the board, play the audio track for Activity 1. Students will hear three speakers give short talks related to the unit topic. Based on what they hear, students should determine if the speaker is talking about his or her experience or opinion.

After playing the audio track once, replay it, but stop after each speaker. Discuss what the students heard (or did not understand), and determine if the speaker was explaining an experience or an opinion. Continue replaying and stopping after each speaker until all three talks have been discussed.

Step 2

Vocabulary and Brainstorming

Have students read through the list of words and phrases as a class, focusing on their pronunciation and meaning. Then have students sort the words and phrases into the three categories provided. After everyone has finished sorting the list, check it as a class. After checking each category, ask students to brainstorm three to five additional words or phrases that could be added to the given category. All of the vocabulary brought out in this activity can help students as they answer the speaking prompts that follow in the unit.

Step 3

Model Dialogs

Play the audio track for Activity 3 and have students read along as they listen. After each dialog, stop the audio and discuss any questions student may have regarding vocabulary or grammar presented in the dialog. After all three dialogs have been heard and discussed, have students work in pairs. Pairs should practice the dialogs, taking turns saying each role.

Note

For classes that need additional pronunciation practice, replay the audio track, but stop after each line or sentence. Students should try to repeat what they hear on the audio track, focusing on their pronunciation and intonation.

Step 4

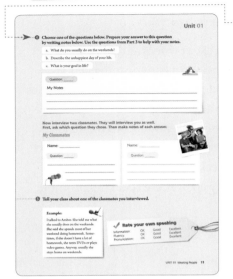

Interviews

Ask each student to choose one of the three questions to answer. Give the students a few minutes to write notes related to how they would answer the question.

Next, assign each student in the class as either "A" or "B." Have students work in A-B pairs. Have the "A" students interview "B" students. First, they should ask which question their classmate chose. "A" students may then refer back to Activity 3 to see possible questions to ask in the interview. Give students two or three minutes to collect information from their partner. Then have the "B" students interview "A" students in the same way.

When these interviews are completed, have all of the "A" students stand up and move to work with a new "B" classmate. Repeat the interview process for the new pairs.

— Note —

Because this activity is an interview, students should not feel pressure to talk at length about their answers during the interviews. Giving one or two sentences as an answer is sufficient for this activity. The interviewer should then ask a follow-up question to get more information from the interviewee until the instructor stops the interview.

Step 5

Reporting

Choose a number of students to report to the class the information they learned through one of their interviews. An example of how students can report information is provided with this activity in each unit.

As an alternative to asking only a few students to report for the class, instructors may divide the class into several groups. Then all members of each group should take turns reporting information they learned through one of their interviews. This way, all of the students in the class can participate in Activity 5.

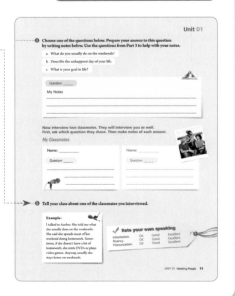

Step 6

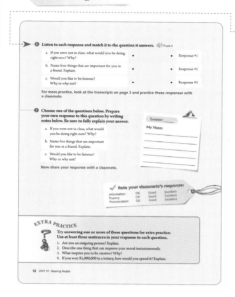

Matching and Modeling

Play the audio track for Activity 6, and have students match the given questions with one of the responses they hear. These questions and responses are meant to provide additional speaking topics and models of responses for students. While checking the answers for this activity, it may be helpful for students to read the responses shown in the transcript for the unit.

— Note —

For classes that need additional pronunciation practice, have students work in pairs reading aloud the sample responses shown in the transcript.

Step 7

Pair Work

Have students work in pairs. One student in each pair will open his/her book. The other student will close his/her book and put it aside for the moment. The student with the open book will choose one of the questions listed in Activity 7 and write notes related to answering the question. The student who does not have a book will be the timer. The timer will look at the board while the instructor marks off increments of 10 seconds on the board. After one minute, the timer tells his/her classmate to stop making notes.

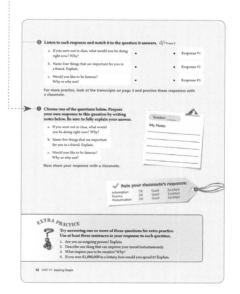

Now it is time for the student with the open book to start talking for two to three minutes (depending on the level of the class). The timer continues watching the board as the instructor marks off increments of time on the board. After the specified time, the timer tells his/her classmate to stop speaking.

The timer will now become the speaker, and the speaker will become the timer. Repeat the above process with the speaker first opening his/her book and making notes for one minute before speaking for two to three minutes.

Step 8

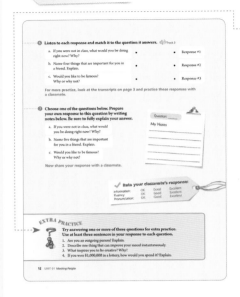

Extra Practice

The questions provided in the Extra Practice activity can be used in a variety of ways. Sometimes, instructors may wish to use these questions for full-class discussions of "hot" topics. Alternatively, the questions can be used for group work or pair work. The questions can also be assigned as journaling homework or speaking homework. As speaking homework, students can record their responses on a voice recorder or using a computer. These responses can be submitted to the instructor for a completion grade or for some other type of evaluation.

--- Note ---

For classes that need additional pronunciation practice, have students work in pairs reading aloud the sample responses shown in the transcript.

Meeting People

1 Listen to the speakers. Check the type of answer the speaker gives.))) Track 1

a. Speaker #1: ☐ personal experience ☐ personal opinion

b. Speaker #2: ☐ personal experience ☐ personal opinion

c. Speaker #3: ☐ personal experience ☐ personal opinion

2 Sort the words and phrases by writing them in the correct categories.

visiting a museum	getting a good education	breaking a bone
the death of a loved one	starting your own company	going hiking
watching a movie	being in an accident	having children
an extended hospital stay	relaxing with friends	owning a home

WEEKEND ACTIVITIES

_____   _____

_____   _____

BAD EVENTS

_____   _____

_____   _____

LIFE GOALS

_____   _____

_____   _____

3 Listen to each dialog and read along. ◁))) Track 2

 WEEKEND ACTIVITIES

A: **What do you usually do on the weekends?**
B: On the weekend, I try to do something exciting or different.
A: **Why do you try and do that?**
B: During the week I work hard and do the same thing every day, so I really try to enjoy my weekends.
A: **What sort of weekend activities do you like?**
B: I like to go hiking, or perhaps visit a museum I haven't been to before.

 BAD EVENTS

A: **Describe the unhappiest day of your life.**
B: The unhappiest day of my life was when I broke my leg.
A: **How did you do that?**
B: It was a really silly accident! I tripped over the sidewalk in my haste to cross the street to get to an ice cream store.
A: **What happened after that?**
B: I had to spend all day in the hospital, and no one came to see me.

 LIFE GOALS

A: **What is your goal in life?**
B: My goal in life is to get a good education, specifically in science.
A: **Why in science?**
B: I want to open my own company to make new medicine to help sick people.
A: **Why do you want to do that?**
B: I believe global health is a very important issue, and people need affordable medicine.

Now practice these dialogs with a classmate.

4 **Choose one of the questions below. Prepare your answer to this question by writing notes below. Use the questions from Part 3 to help with your notes.**

a. What do you usually do on the weekends?

b. Describe the unhappiest day of your life.

c. What is your goal in life?

Question: _____

My Notes

_____

_____

_____

Now interview two classmates. They will interview you as well. First, ask which question they chose. Then make notes of each answer.

My Classmates

Name: _____

Question: _____

_____

_____

Name: _____

Question: _____

_____

_____

5 **Tell your class about one of the classmates you interviewed.**

Example:

I talked to Amber. She told me what she usually does on the weekends. She said she spends most of her weekend doing homework. Sometimes, if she doesn't have a lot of homework, she rents DVDs or plays video games. Anyway, she usually stays home on weekends.

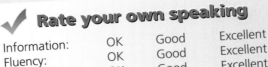

✔ **Rate your own speaking**

Information:	OK	Good	Excellent
Fluency:	OK	Good	Excellent
Pronunciation:	OK	Good	Excellent

6 **Listen to each response and match it to the question it answers.** 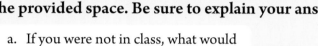 **Track 3**

a. If you were not in class, what would you be doing right now? Why?

b. What are some important qualities in a friend?

c. Would you like to be famous? Why or why not?

• • Response #1

• • Response #2

• • Response #3

For more practice, look at the transcripts on page 1 and practice these responses with a classmate.

7 **Choose one of the questions below. Prepare your own response to this question by writing notes in the provided space. Be sure to explain your answer.**

a. If you were not in class, what would you be doing right now? Why?

b. What are some important qualities in a friend?

c. Would you like to be famous? Why or why not?

Now share your response with a classmate.

Question: _____

My Notes

_____

_____

_____

_____

_____

Rate your classmate's response:

	OK	Good	Excellent
Information:	OK	Good	Excellent
Fluency:	OK	Good	Excellent
Pronunciation:	OK	Good	Excellent

 **EXTRA PRACTICE**

 Try answering one or more of these questions for extra practice. Use at least three sentences in your response to each question.

1. Are you an outgoing person? Explain.
2. Describe one thing that can improve your mood instantaneously.
3. What inspires you to be creative? Why?
4. If you won $1,000,000 in a lottery, how would you spend it? Explain.

Sports

1 **Listen to the speakers. Check the type of answer the speaker gives.** 🔊 Track 4

a. Speaker #1: ☐ personal experience ☐ personal opinion

b. Speaker #2: ☐ personal experience ☐ personal opinion

c. Speaker #3: ☐ personal experience ☐ personal opinion

2 **Sort the words and phrases by writing them in the correct categories.**

attend many games	can enhance performance	is an old sport
are illegal	collect memorabilia	played by fat men
traditional sport of Japan	give an unfair advantage	follow favorite teams
used by some athletes	matches are over quickly	know about players

🏆 **SUMO WRESTLING**

_____ _____

_____ _____

SPORTS FANS

_____ _____

_____ _____

DRUGS IN SPORTS

_____ _____

_____ _____

3 **Listen to each dialog and read along.** 🔊 Track 5

SUMO WRESTLING

A: **What is a traditional sport of your country?**

B: Sumo is a traditional sport of my country. It's an old sport filled with rituals.

A: **Describe it.**

B: The aim is to get your opponent out of the ring or on the ground.

A: **What are sumo wrestlers like?**

B: Sumo wrestlers are normally fat, powerful men.

SPORTS FANS

A: **Are you a sports fan?**

B: No, I'm not a sports fan the way I understand it.

A: **Who's a real sports fan?**

B: To be a real sports fan, you have to attend all the games of your favorite team, know everything about its players, and collect memorabilia of your team.

A: **Do you have a favorite sports team?**

B: I don't do all that, but I have a favorite team. They are not the best team, but they have the most heart.

DRUGS IN SPORTS

A: **Do you think athletes should be allowed to take drugs to enhance their performance?**

B: No, I think taking drugs to enhance performance is immoral. It is also illegal.

A: **Why do you feel that way?**

B: Using drugs gives an athlete an unfair advantage over other players.

A: **What's the worst thing about these drugs?**

B: Even worse, drugs can have serious negative effects on an athlete's health.

Now practice these dialogs with a classmate.

4 Choose one of the questions below. Prepare your answer to this question by writing notes below. Use the questions from Part 3 to help with your notes.

a. What is a traditional sport of your country? Describe it.

b. Are you a sports fan? What is your favorite team?

c. Do you think athletes should be allowed to take drugs to enhance their performance? Explain.

Question: _____

My Notes

_____

_____

_____

Now interview two classmates. They will interview you as well. First, ask which question they chose. Then make notes of each answer.

My Classmates

Name: _____

Question: _____

_____

_____

_____

Name: _____

Question: _____

_____

_____

_____

5 Tell your class about one of the classmates you interviewed.

Example:

I talked to Bill. He said that he is a baseball fan. He hasn't been to a baseball game in a while, but he said he enjoys watching them when he has a chance. His favorite team is the Bears. Bill said he has been a Bears fan ever since he was a kid.

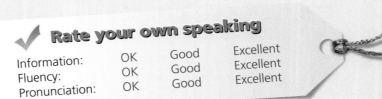

Rate your own speaking

	OK	Good	Excellent
Information:	OK	Good	Excellent
Fluency:	OK	Good	Excellent
Pronunciation:	OK	Good	Excellent

6 **Listen to each response and match it to the question it answers.** 🔊 **Track 6**

a. What sport do you enjoy watching on TV? Describe it. •

• Response #1

b. How do injuries influence professional athletes' careers and lives? •

• Response #2

c. Do you think that there are some sports that are inappropriate for women to play? Explain. •

• Response #3

For more practice, look at the transcripts on page 1 and practice these responses with a classmate.

7 **Choose one of the questions below. Prepare your own response to this question by writing notes in the provided space. Be sure to explain your answer.**

a. What sport do you enjoy watching on TV? Describe it.

b. How do injuries influence professional athletes' careers and lives?

c. Do you think that there are some sports that are inappropriate for women to play? Explain.

Now share your response with a classmate.

Question: _____

My Notes

_____

_____

_____

_____

_____

Rate your classmate's response:

Information:	OK	Good	Excellent
Fluency:	OK	Good	Excellent
Pronunciation:	OK	Good	Excellent

EXTRA PRACTICE

Try answering one or more of these questions for extra practice. Use at least three sentences in your response to each question.

1. Who is your favorite basketball player?
2. Do you think hunting and fishing are sports? Explain.
3. Why do you think professional athletes change teams frequently?
4. Should advertising companies use professional athletes to promote their products? Explain.

Friendship

1 **Listen to the speakers. Check the type of answer the speaker gives.** Track 7

a. Speaker #1: ☐ personal experience ☐ personal opinion

b. Speaker #2: ☐ personal experience ☐ personal opinion

c. Speaker #3: ☐ personal experience ☐ personal opinion

2 **Sort the words and phrases by writing them in the correct categories.**

makes you laugh	at school	at church	talk through email
at a party	enjoys the same activities	stay in contact	in a club
cares about you	similar interests	talk on the phone	lots of effort

ATTRIBUTES OF A BEST FRIEND

_____   _____

_____   _____

PLACES TO MEET

_____   _____

_____   _____

LONG-DISTANCE FRIENDSHIPS

_____   _____

_____   _____

3 Listen to each dialog and read along. **Track 8**

ATTRIBUTES OF A BEST FRIEND

A: **Describe your best friend.**

B: He always makes me laugh, but at the same time, he really cares about me.

A: **Why is he your best friend?**

B: He is my best friend because we have so many similar interests.

A: **Have you been friends for a long time?**

B: We've been friends ever since we first met each other in elementary school.

MEETING NEW FRIENDS

A: **Where do you think is a good place to meet new friends?**

B: I think the best place to meet friends is in a school club or social club.

A: **What should you look for in a new friend?**

B: It is always easier to become friends with someone with whom you have something in common.

A: **Is it important to be comfortable when meeting a new friend?**

B: Yes, a place where you are comfortable and where you have fun is also a great place to meet new friends.

LONG-DISTANCE FRIENDSHIPS

A: **Do you think it is possible to maintain a long-distance friendship?**

B: Of course, it is possible to have a long-distance relationship.

A: **What is the best way to communicate?**

B: With the Internet, it is so easy to stay in contact with people. You can call or email them nearly everyday.

A: **What is needed from the people involved?**

B: As long as both friends are willing to put in the little bit of extra effort to stay in contact, there is no reason why the friendship cannot work.

Now practice these dialogs with a classmate.

4 Choose one of the questions below. Prepare your answer to this question by writing notes below. Use the questions from Part 3 to help with your notes.

a. Describe your best friend.

b. Where do you think is a good place to meet new friends?

c. Do you think it is possible to maintain a long-distance friendship?

Question: _____

My Notes

_____

_____

_____

Now interview two classmates. They will interview you as well. First, ask which question they chose. Then make notes of each answer.

My Classmates

Name: _____

Question: _____

_____

_____

_____

Name: _____

Question: _____

_____

_____

_____

5 Tell your class about one of the classmates you interviewed.

Example:

I talked to Cindy. She thinks that it is possible to maintain a long-distance friendship. In fact, she told me about a friend she has in Australia. She has never met this friend in person. It is someone she met through a pen pal club. They have been friends for about three years.

✔ **Rate your own speaking**

Information:	OK	Good	Excellent
Fluency:	OK	Good	Excellent
Pronunciation:	OK	Good	Excellent

6 Listen to each response and match it to the question it answers. Track 9

a. Do you think it is possible to be friends with people who are much older than you are?

b. How might your friends influence you in a negative way? Explain.

c. Explain the saying "Tell me who your friends are, and I will tell you who you are"?

Response #1

Response #2

Response #3

For more practice, look at the transcripts on page 2 and practice these responses with a classmate.

7 Choose one of the questions below. Prepare your own response to this question by writing notes in the provided space. Be sure to explain your answer.

a. Do you think it is possible to be friends with people who are much older than you are?

b. How might your friends influence you in a negative way? Explain.

c. Explain the saying "Tell me who your friends are, and I will tell you who you are"?

Now share your response with a classmate.

Question: _____

My Notes

_____
_____
_____
_____
_____

 Rate your classmate's response:

	OK	Good	Excellent
Information:	OK	Good	Excellent
Fluency:	OK	Good	Excellent
Pronunciation:	OK	Good	Excellent

EXTRA PRACTICE

Try answering one or more of these questions for extra practice. Use at least three sentences in your response to each question.

1. Explain the proverb "A friend in need is a friend indeed."
2. Do you agree with the following saying "Books and friends should be few but good"? Explain.
3. What does the Chinese proverb "Do not remove a fly from your friend's forehead with a hatchet" mean?
4. Explain the Spanish proverb "It is better to weep with wise men than to laugh with fools."

Holidays

1 **Listen to the speakers. Check the type of answer the speaker gives.** 🔊 Track 10

a. Speaker #1: ☐ personal experience ☐ personal opinion

b. Speaker #2: ☐ personal experience ☐ personal opinion

c. Speaker #3: ☐ personal experience ☐ personal opinion

2 **Sort the words and phrases by writing them in the correct categories.**

big feast	box of chocolates	promotions	roses
dinner date	everyone comes home	catch up	sales
commercial	romantic	profits	traditional foods

A FAMILY GET TOGETHER

_____   _____

_____   _____

VALENTINE'S DAY

_____   _____

_____   _____

BUSINESSES

_____   _____

_____   _____

3 Listen to each dialog and read along. Track 11

A FAMILY GET TOGETHER

A: **Do people celebrate Thanksgiving in your country or culture?**

B: Yes, we celebrate Thanksgiving.

A: **How do you celebrate it?**

B: We always go to our grandparents' house and have a big feast.

A: **What do you eat and what do you do?**

B: We enjoy traditional dishes, sit around and catch up with all of our relatives, and see how their lives are going.

VALENTINE'S DAY

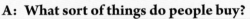

A: **Describe how you celebrate Valentine's Day in your country or culture.**

B: Valentine's day is a huge holiday in my country. You see hearts, chocolate, and roses for sale everywhere.

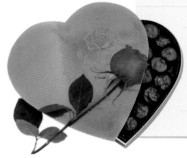

A: **What sort of things do people buy?**

B: People go out for dinner and exchange gifts, like boxes of chocolates, flowers, and cards.

A: **Is it a romantic day?**

B: It is supposed to be a really romantic holiday, but I think it's all just a waste of money.

BUSINESSES

A: **How do businesses make money on holidays?**

B: Businesses make money through promotion and sales of specialty items specifically designed for the holiday.

A: **Do you think holidays are becoming too commercialized?**

B: The big holidays have become too commercialized these days, so they're not really fun anymore.

A: **What about minor holidays?**

B: Because they make so much money, businesses have started to promote even minor holidays in hopes of making a profit.

Now practice these dialogs with a classmate.

4 **Choose one of the questions below. Prepare your answer to this question by writing notes below. Use the questions from Part 3 to help with your notes.**

a. Do people celebrate Thanksgiving in your country/culture?

b. Describe how you celebrate Valentine's Day in your country/culture.

c. How do businesses make money on holidays?

Question: _____

My Notes

_____

_____

_____

Now interview two classmates. They will interview you as well. First, ask which question they chose. Then make notes of each answer.

My Classmates

Name: _____

Question: _____

_____

_____

_____

Name: _____

Question: _____

_____

_____

5 **Tell your class about one of the classmates you interviewed.**

Example:

I talked to David. He explained how people in his country celebrate Thanksgiving. On Thanksgiving Day, family members gather at someone's house, and they all eat a big meal. It sounds a lot like the way they celebrate Thanksgiving here. David said that he usually watches TV or plays cards after the meal.

✔ Rate your own speaking

	OK	Good	Excellent
Information:	OK	Good	Excellent
Fluency:	OK	Good	Excellent
Pronunciation:	OK	Good	Excellent

6 Listen to each response and match it to the question it answers. Track 12

a. What is one of the most important holidays in your country/culture?

b. Describe a childhood memory of celebrating a holiday with your family.

c. Describe a special holiday meal that you have prepared or eaten.

• • Response #1

• • Response #2

• • Response #3

For more practice, look at the transcripts on page 2 and practice these responses with a classmate.

7 Choose one of the questions below. Prepare your own response to this question by writing notes in the provided space. Be sure to explain your answer.

a. What is one of the most important holidays in your country/culture?

b. Describe a childhood memory of celebrating a holiday with your family.

c. Describe a special holiday meal that you have prepared or eaten.

Now share your response with a classmate.

Question: _____

My Notes

_____
_____
_____
_____
_____

✔ Rate your classmate's response:

	OK	Good	Excellent
Information:	OK	Good	Excellent
Fluency:	OK	Good	Excellent
Pronunciation:	OK	Good	Excellent

EXTRA PRACTICE

Try answering one or more of these questions for extra practice. Use at least three sentences in your response to each question.

1. How do you celebrate birthdays in your family?
2. Is there a Teacher's Day in your country/culture?
3. What is your opinion about making New Year's resolutions?
4. When do you celebrate a Mother's or Women's Day in your country/culture?

Stereotypes

1 **Listen to the speakers. Check the type of answer the speaker gives.** 🔊 Track 13

   a. Speaker #1:   ☐ personal experience   ☐ personal opinion

   b. Speaker #2:   ☐ personal experience   ☐ personal opinion

   c. Speaker #3:   ☐ personal experience   ☐ personal opinion

2 **Sort the words and phrases by writing them in the correct categories.**

faithful wife	construction worker	masculine
stronger than women	caretaker of the house	good cook
machine operator	housekeeper	swears a lot
enjoys physical labor	mechanic	fisherman

STEREOTYPICAL WOMEN'S ROLES

_____ _____

_____ _____

PHYSICAL JOBS

_____ _____

_____ _____

THE STEREOTYPICAL MAN

_____ _____

_____ _____

3 Listen to each dialog and read along. 🔊 Track 14

STEREOTYPICAL WOMEN'S ROLES

A: What is the typical woman's role in a family in your culture?

B: The typical woman's role in a family in my culture is a faithful wife, caring mother, and good cook.

A: Why are women expected to take on this role?

B: I think women are expected to do all these things because it is what they have traditionally done.

A: What are women mainly responsible for in your culture?

B: It is often seen as the woman's responsibility to be the caretaker of the house.

PHYSICAL JOBS

A: What are typical jobs or occupations for men in your culture?

B: Most jobs that deal with physical labor such as construction and stuff typically belong to men.

A: Can you think of any other examples?

B: Mechanics and heavy machinery operators tend also to be men.

A: Why are these jobs considered for males only?

B: I think that these jobs are typically male jobs because they involve a lot of dirt, sweat, and pain, which are things that are often embraced in a male culture.

THE STEREOTYPICAL MAN

A: What language or vocabulary is considered appropriate for a man to use but inappropriate for a woman in your culture?

B: In my culture, it is OK for men to swear or use strong language. It is not seen as a big deal by most people.

A: What about women?

B: Women who swear in public are often labeled as uncouth or unladylike.

A: Why is that?

B: This is because women have traditionally been seen as pleasant and soft-spoken.

Now practice these dialogs with a classmate.

4 **Choose one of the questions below. Prepare your answer to this question by writing notes below. Use the questions from Part 3 to help with your notes.**

a. What is the typical woman's role in a family in your culture?

b. What are typical jobs/occupations for men in your culture?

c. What language/vocabulary is considered appropriate for a man to use but inappropriate for a woman in your culture?

Question: _____

My Notes

_____

_____

_____

Now interview two classmates. They will interview you as well. First, ask which question they chose. Then make notes of each answer.

My Classmates

Name: _____

Question: _____

_____

_____

_____

Name: _____

Question: _____

_____

_____

5 **Tell your class about one of the classmates you interviewed.**

Example:

I talked to Ellen. She told me about the typical jobs that men in her family have. She said her uncles and male cousins mostly work in large international companies. She didn't say exactly what they do. They just have office jobs.

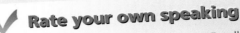

✔ **Rate your own speaking**

Information:	OK	Good	Excellent
Fluency:	OK	Good	Excellent
Pronunciation:	OK	Good	Excellent

6 **Listen to each response and match it to the question it answers.** 🔊 Track15

a. Whose responsibility is it to take care of children in your culture? Why?

b. Do you think a father can raise a daughter alone, without a woman's help? Explain.

c. Give examples of sports in your culture that only men can compete in.

•   • Response #1

•   • Response #2

•   • Response #3

For more practice, look at the transcripts on page 3 and practice these responses with a classmate.

7 **Choose one of the questions below. Prepare your own response to this question by writing notes in the provided space. Be sure to explain your answer.**

a. Whose responsibility is it to take care of children in your culture? Why?

b. Do you think a father can raise a daughter alone, without a woman's help? Explain.

c. Give examples of sports in your culture that only men can compete in.

Now share your response with a classmate.

Question: _____

My Notes

_____

_____

_____

_____

_____

✔ **Rate your classmate's response:**

	OK	Good	Excellent
Information:	OK	Good	Excellent
Fluency:	OK	Good	Excellent
Pronunciation:	OK	Good	Excellent

EXTRA PRACTICE

Try answering one or more of these questions for extra practice. Use at least three sentences in your response to each question.

1. What colors are acceptable for a woman to wear but are unacceptable for a man? Explain.
2. Can a woman be a "breadwinner" in your culture? Explain.
3. Is it acceptable for a woman or man to show strong emotions in public? Explain.
4. How is a certain body image formed and promoted in society?

Time Management

1 Listen to the speakers. Check the type of answer the speaker gives. )) Track 16

a. Speaker #1:   ☐ personal experience   ☐ personal opinion

b. Speaker #2:   ☐ personal experience   ☐ personal opinion

c. Speaker #3:   ☐ personal experience   ☐ personal opinion

2 Sort the words and phrases by writing them in the correct categories.

keep track of deadlines	attending lectures	usually in bed
during the night	important events	studying
upcoming assignments	a time for resting	reading
close your eyes	taking notes	appointments

🕐 DAILY PLANNING

_____   _____

_____   _____

🎓 SCHOOLWORK

_____   _____

_____   _____

☾ SLEEP

_____   _____

_____   _____

3 **Listen to each dialog and read along.** Track 17

DAILY PLANNING

A: **Is it important to keep a daily planner, calendar, or a PDA?**

B: Yes, it is important to use a planner of some sort.

A: **Why is it important?**

B: It's helpful to have something that helps you keep track of your deadlines and upcoming assignments.

A: **Do you have one?**

B: I like using a wall calendar because I can make note of important events and see everything that I need to accomplish this month at a glance.

SCHOOLWORK

A: **How could you minimize the time that you spend doing your homework, studying, and reading?**

B: I could minimize the time by paying attention at school and taking notes of my teachers' lectures.

A: **How does paying attention help you?**

B: When I pay attention at school, I learn much faster and better.

A: **Does that make it easier for you?**

B: I find it much easier to remember and understand the information we have been given.

SLEEP

A: **How much time do you spend sleeping?**

B: I usually sleep for about 6-7 hours each night.

A: **Is it enough?**

B: I don't think it's enough because I always have difficulty waking up in the morning and staying awake in my first class.

A: **Would you like to spend more or less time sleeping?**

B: I would love to stay in bed longer, but I also think there are not enough hours in the day to do all the things I need to do.

Now practice these dialogs with a classmate.

4 **Choose one of the questions below. Prepare your answer to this question by writing notes below. Use the questions from Part 3 to help with your notes.**

    a. Is it important to keep a daily planner, calendar, or a PDA?

    b. How could you minimize the time that you spend doing your homework, studying, and reading?

    c. How much time do you spend sleeping?

Question: _____

My Notes

_____

_____

_____

Now interview two classmates. They will interview you as well. First, ask which question they chose. Then make notes of each answer.

My Classmates

Name: _____

Question: _____

_____

_____

_____

Name: _____

Question: _____

_____

_____

_____

5 **Tell your class about one of the classmates you interviewed.**

Example:

I talked to Fred. He told me how much time he spends sleeping. He said that during the week he usually sleeps about six hours each night. He studies or works at night until about 1 a.m. Then he wakes up at 7 a.m. to get ready for classes. Usually on weekends he sleeps eight to ten hours per night.

Rate your own speaking

	OK	Good	Excellent
Information:	OK	Good	Excellent
Fluency:	OK	Good	Excellent
Pronunciation:	OK	Good	Excellent

6 **Listen to each response and match it to the question it answers.** 🔊 **Track 18**

a. Why do you think it is important to manage your time wisely?

b. How much time do you spend at school (at work) every day? Is it too much or too little? Explain.

c. How much time do you spend browsing the Internet? Do you think it is too much? Explain.

• Response #1

• Response #2

• Response #3

For more practice, look at the transcripts on page 4 and practice these responses with a classmate.

7 **Choose one of the questions below. Prepare your own response to this question by writing notes in the provided space. Be sure to explain your answer.**

a. Why do you think it is important to manage your time wisely?

b. How much time do you spend at school (at work) every day? Is it too much or too little? Explain.

c. How much time do you spend browsing the Internet? Do you think it is too much? Explain.

Now share your response with a classmate.

Question: _____

My Notes

_____
_____
_____
_____
_____

✔ Rate your classmate's response:

Information:	OK	Good	Excellent
Fluency:	OK	Good	Excellent
Pronunciation:	OK	Good	Excellent

EXTRA PRACTICE

Try answering one or more of these questions for extra practice. Use at least three sentences in your response to each question.

1. Give examples of things that make you waste a lot of time.
2. Do you procrastinate? Give examples of how and when you procrastinate.
3. If your friend invites you for a birthday party, is it OK to be late? Explain.
4. Explain the saying "The early bird gets the worm."

Schooling

1 **Listen to the speakers. Check the type of answer the speaker gives.** 🔊 Track 19

    a. Speaker #1:   ☐ personal experience   ☐ personal opinion

    b. Speaker #2:   ☐ personal experience   ☐ personal opinion

    c. Speaker #3:   ☐ personal experience   ☐ personal opinion

2 **Sort the words and phrases by writing them in the correct categories.**

can hurt your eyes	fit in with peers	slower paced learning
develop social skills	carpal tunnel syndrome	harmful for kids
no face-to-face interaction	study areas you like	flexible schedule
communicate with teachers	fits your own learning style	access to school facilities

🏠 **HOME SCHOOLING ADVANTAGES**

_____   _____

_____   _____

🏛 **PUBLIC SCHOOL ADVANTAGES**

_____   _____

_____   _____

💻 **COMPUTER DISADVANTAGES**

_____   _____

_____   _____

3 **Listen to each dialog and read along.** 🔊 Track 20

🏠 HOME SCHOOLING ADVANTAGES

A: **What are the advantages of being schooled at home?**

B: For one thing, you can concentrate on learning the things you are interested in. You can also learn at your own pace.

A: **What about a student's learning style?**

B: When kids are taught at home, their parents can tap into the learning style that best suits the student.

A: **How is home schooling flexible?**

B: Home schooling is flexible with regard to when classes start or stop, how long they are, and even which subjects to study each day.

🏛 PUBLIC SCHOOL ADVANTAGES

A: **What important skills do children acquire in public schools?**

B: Besides studying, children also acquire important social skills that help them fit in with their peers.

A: **Is it important to fit in with peers?**

B: Students need to learn how to fit in so that later in life they will know how to interact with others in work or social situations.

A: **How does a student develop perseverance?**

B: In regular school, students learn to persevere even when classes or programs seem really hard for them.

💻 COMPUTER DISADVANTAGES

A: **Do you think it could be harmful for children to spend a lot of time in front of their computers?**

B: Yes, spending too much time in front of the computer can be harmful for children.

A: **What disabilities may develop with computer overuse?**

B: Constant exposure to computer screens can hurt children's eyes. It can also potentially lead to things like carpal tunnel syndrome.

A: **Is face-to-face communication important? Why?**

B: Children need to learn to interact face-to-face with other people to be functioning adults.

Now practice these dialogs with a classmate.

4 **Choose one of the questions below. Prepare your answer to this question by writing notes below. Use the questions from Part 3 to help with your notes.**

a. What are the advantages of being schooled at home?

b. What important skills do children acquire in public schools?

c. Do you think it might be harmful for children to spend a lot of time in front of their computers?

Question: _____

My Notes

_____

_____

_____

Now interview two classmates. They will interview you as well. First, ask which question they chose. Then make notes of each answer.

My Classmates

Name: _____

Question: _____

_____

_____

 _____

Name: _____

Question: _____

_____

_____

_____

5 **Tell your class about one of the classmates you interviewed.**

Example:

I talked to Grace. She explained an advantage to home schooling. She said the biggest advantage is that kids can more easily connect their lessons to things in their lives. For example, if they study math, they can focus the math lesson on real-life things related to the family.

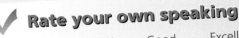

Rate your own speaking

	OK	Good	Excellent
Information:	OK	Good	Excellent
Fluency:	OK	Good	Excellent
Pronunciation:	OK	Good	Excellent

6 Listen to each response and match it to the question it answers. 🔊 Track 21

    a. What are some of the disadvantages of public schooling?   •   • Response #1

    b. What are the advantages and disadvantages of student-teacher interactions? Explain.   •   • Response #2

    c. How might home-schooled children have difficulty in social situations when they grow up? Explain.   •   • Response #3

For more practice, look at the transcripts on page 4 and practice these responses with a classmate.

7 **Choose one of the questions below. Prepare your own response to this question by writing notes in the provided space. Be sure to explain your answer.**

    a. What are some of the disadvantages of public schooling?

    b. What are the advantages and disadvantages of student-teacher interactions? Explain.

    c. How might home-schooled children have difficulty in social situations when they grow up? Explain.

Now share your response with a classmate.

Question: _____

My Notes
_____
_____
_____
_____
_____

✔ Rate your classmate's response:

	OK	Good	Excellent
Information:	OK	Good	Excellent
Fluency:	OK	Good	Excellent
Pronunciation:	OK	Good	Excellent

EXTRA PRACTICE

Try answering one or more of these questions for extra practice. Use at least three sentences in your response to each question.

1. Where do you think children experience more peer pressure: through homeschooling or public schooling?
2. What can children do when they have difficulty studying or doing homework?
3. What is your opinion: will more children be schooled at home in the future or not?
4. Describe parent-child interaction when a child starts going to public school.

Politics

1 **Listen to the speakers. Check the type of answer the speaker gives.** Track 22

   a. Speaker #1: ☐ personal experience ☐ personal opinion

   b. Speaker #2: ☐ personal experience ☐ personal opinion

   c. Speaker #3: ☐ personal experience ☐ personal opinion

2 **Sort the words and phrases by writing them in the correct categories.**

monarchies	courts	use weapons
wear uniforms	democracies	dictatorships
judges	lawyers	have soldiers
do peacekeeping	appeals	republics

GOVERNMENTS

_____ _____

_____ _____

LEGAL MATTERS

_____ _____

_____ _____

ARMIES

_____ _____

_____ _____

3 **Listen to each dialog and read along.** 🔊 Track 23

GOVERNMENTS

A: **Describe various forms of government that exist nowadays.**

B: Some of the forms of government that exist today are monarchies, democracies, dictatorships, and republics.

A: **Which do you find to be the most interesting form of government?**

B: I find monarchies to be the oldest and the most interesting form of government of our time.

A: **Why do you feel that way?**

B: Monarchies combine the ancient traditions of royalty with modern forms of government.

LEGAL MATTERS

A: **What is the highest court in your country?**

B: The highest court in my country is called the Supreme Court.

A: **What kinds of crime does it normally deal with?**

B: It is responsible for ruling on appeals to difficult or controversial legal cases that lower courts reached decisions about.

A: **Is the Supreme Court the last step in legal procedures?**

B: Yes, it is responsible for the final decision in the legal process.

ARMIES

A: **Why do you think countries need armies?**

B: Countries need armies because they represent power and ensure national and international security.

A: **Is there a mandatory army service in your country?**

B: Army service is not compulsory in my country.

A: **Does the army of your country do any work internationally?**

B: Although my country has a small army, it contributes to international security by sending soldiers on peacekeeping missions to several countries.

Now practice these dialogs with a classmate.

4 **Choose one of the questions below. Prepare your answer to this question by writing notes below. Use the questions from Part 3 to help with your notes.**

  a. Describe various forms of government that exist nowadays and give examples of countries that have these governments.

  b. What is the highest court in your country, and what kind of decisions does it make?

  c. Why do you think countries need armies?

Question: _____

My Notes

_____

_____

_____

Now interview two classmates. They will interview you as well. First, ask which question they chose. Then make notes of each answer.

My Classmates

Name: _____

Question: _____

_____

_____

_____

Name: _____

Question: _____

_____

_____

_____

5 **Tell your class about one of the classmates you interviewed.**

Example:

I talked to Harry. He told me about the highest court in his country. The highest court in his country is called the Supreme Court. That court hears important cases that can have a great effect on the laws of the country.

✔ **Rate your own speaking**

Information:	OK	Good	Excellent
Fluency:	OK	Good	Excellent
Pronunciation:	OK	Good	Excellent

6 Listen to each response and match it to the question it answers. Track 24

a. Who is the official ruler of your country?
What power does he or she have?

• • Response #1

b. Have you ever had a female president in your country? If so, tell us about her. If not, explain why.

• • Response #2

c. What political offices in your country do people elect? How frequent are the elections? What is the election process like?

• • Response #3

For more practice, look at the transcripts on page 5 and practice these responses with a classmate.

7 Choose one of the questions below. Prepare your own response to this question by writing notes in the provided space. Be sure to explain your answer.

a. Who is the official ruler of your country?
What power does he or she have?

b. Have you ever had a female president in your country? If so, tell us about her. If not, explain why.

c. What political offices in your country do people elect? How frequent are the elections? What is the election process like?

Question: _____

My Notes

_____

_____

_____

_____

_____

Now share your response with a classmate.

✓ Rate your classmate's response:

Information:	OK	Good	Excellent
Fluency:	OK	Good	Excellent
Pronunciation:	OK	Good	Excellent

 EXTRA PRACTICE

Try answering one or more of these questions for extra practice. Use at least three sentences in your response to each question.

1. What is the structure of the government in your country?
2. Which branch of the government is responsible for enforcing the laws?
3. Who is the chief commander of the army in your country?
4. Do people actively participate in elections in your country? Explain.

If You Could

1 **Listen to the speakers. Check the type of answer the speaker gives.** 🔊 Track 25

a. Speaker #1: ☐ personal experience ☐ personal opinion

b. Speaker #2: ☐ personal experience ☐ personal opinion

c. Speaker #3: ☐ personal experience ☐ personal opinion

2 **Sort the words and phrases by writing them in the correct categories.**

elephants	play volleyball	on the big screen	in a theater
go swimming	rhinos	giraffes	get a sun tan
hyenas	have a massage	sometimes emotional	surround sound

SAFARI ANIMALS

_____ _____

_____ _____

A BEACH VACATION

_____ _____

_____ _____

MOVIES

_____ _____

_____ _____

3 **Listen to each dialog and read along.** 🔊)) Track 26

SAFARI ANIMALS

A: **If you got a chance, where would you go on vacation?**
B: If I had the chance, I would go to Tanzania for vacation.
A: **Why would you go there?**
B: I could go on a safari and see wild elephants, rhinos, and giraffes.
A: **What would you do there?**
B: I could visit the ancient city of Zanzibar, and I could also relax on a beautiful beach and just sit back and relax.

A BEACH VACATION

A: **If you got a chance, where would you be now?**
B: If I had the chance, I would be at the beach with my friends now.
A: **What would you do there?**
B: We would play volleyball, swim, and have fun because I am tired of studying and working hard.
A: **Why would you go there?**
B: I need to reduce the stress and anxiety of everyday life. Being at the beach would be great.

MOVIES

A: **If you got a chance, what movie would you watch again?**
B: If I had the chance, I would watch the movie *Life is Beautiful*.
A: **What's the movie about?**
B: It is a story about a man in a concentration camp during World War II.
A: **What's the theme of the movie?**
B: The movie's theme is to make the best of a situation no matter how grim it is.

Now practice these dialogs with a classmate.

4 **Choose one of the questions below. Prepare your answer to this question by writing notes below. Use the questions from Part 3 to help with your notes.**

a. If you got a chance, where would you go on vacation?

b. If you got a chance, where would you be now?

c. If you got a chance, what movies would you watch again?

Question: _____

My Notes

_____

_____

_____

Now interview two classmates. They will interview you as well. First, ask which question they chose. Then make notes of each answer.

My Classmates

Name: _____

Question: _____

_____

_____

_____

Name: _____

Question: _____

_____

_____

5 **Tell your class about one of the classmates you interviewed.**

Example:

I talked to Inez. She told me about a movie that she would like to watch again if she got the chance. She said she wants to see the movie *Gone With the Wind* again. She said the story is very interesting and the scenes are beautiful. I don't know. I've never seen it.

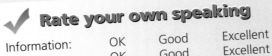

✔ **Rate your own speaking**

Information:	OK	Good	Excellent
Fluency:	OK	Good	Excellent
Pronunciation:	OK	Good	Excellent

6 **Listen to each response and match it to the question it answers.**  Track 27

a. If you got a chance, what sort of house would you live in? Explain.

b. If you got a chance, what kind of car would you buy? Explain.

c. If you got a chance, what language would you study? Explain.

• Response #1

• Response #2

• Response #3

For more practice, look at the transcripts on page 5 and practice these responses with a classmate.

7 **Choose one of the questions below. Prepare your own response to this question by writing notes in the provided space. Be sure to explain your answer.**

a. If you got a chance, what sort of house would you live in? Explain.

b. If you got a chance, what kind of car would you buy? Explain.

c. If you got a chance, what language would you study? Explain.

Now share your response with a classmate.

Question: _____

My Notes

_____
_____
_____
_____
_____

✔ **Rate your classmate's response:**

Information:	OK	Good	Excellent
Fluency:	OK	Good	Excellent
Pronunciation:	OK	Good	Excellent

EXTRA PRACTICE

Try answering one or more of these questions for extra practice. Use at least three sentences in your response to each question.

1. If you got a chance, what celebrity would you like to meet? Explain.
2. If you had a chance, what subjects would you study? Why?
3. If you got a chance, what would you change about your life? Explain.
4. If you had a chance, what would you have done differently? Explain.

Inventions and Discoveries

1 **Listen to the speakers. Check the type of answer the speaker gives.** Track 28

a. Speaker #1: ☐ personal experience ☐ personal opinion

b. Speaker #2: ☐ personal experience ☐ personal opinion

c. Speaker #3: ☐ personal experience ☐ personal opinion

2 **Sort the words and phrases by writing them in the correct categories.**

birds	telescopes	destroys infections
cameras	fights diseases	fights bacterial infection
exploration	planet watching	airplanes
hot air balloons	helps people recover	helicopters

THINGS THAT FLY

_____ _____

_____ _____

STUDYING SPACE

_____ _____

_____ _____

PENICILLIN

_____ _____

_____ _____

3 **Listen to each dialog and read along.** 🔊 Track 29

✈ THINGS THAT FLY

A: **What do you know about the invention of flight?**
B: At first, people used balloons to fly.
A: **Describe the evolution of the airplane.**
B: It wasn't until 1903 when Wilbur and Orville Wright successfully flew the first man-powered machine.
A: **How long was the flight?**
B: Their flight was short, but it would soon lead to rapid changes in aviation.

☾ STUDYING SPACE

A: **What inventions are necessary for space travel?**
B: The most important invention for space travel is the ability to travel at the speed of light.
A: **What do you think is the future for space exploration?**
B: The future of space exploration lies on Mars. It is the only planet that is close enough to establish any sort of exploration on.
A: **What other options do we have?**
B: Other than that, we will have to continue exploring space through telescopes and cameras.

💉 PENICILLIN

A: **Describe an important advancement in the field of medicine.**
B: The most important advancement in modern medicine was penicillin.
A: **What does it do?**
B: Post-surgical infections are as dangerous as the actual disease itself. Penicillin destroys many of these infections.
A: **Why is this advancement so important?**
B: Without penicillin, other medical advancements in surgery would have been impossible, which is why penicillin is the most important.

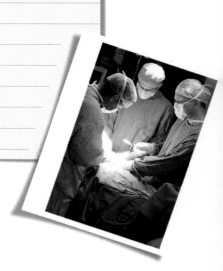

Now practice these dialogs with a classmate.

4 **Choose one of the questions below. Prepare your answer to this question by writing notes below. Use the questions from Part 3 to help with your notes.**

a. What do you know about the invention of flight?

b. What inventions are necessary for space travel?

c. Describe an important advancement in the field of medicine.

Question: _____

My Notes

_____

_____

_____

Now interview two classmates. They will interview you as well. First, ask which question they chose. Then make notes of each answer.

My Classmates

Name: _____

Question: _____

_____

_____

_____

Name: _____

Question: _____

_____

_____

_____

5 **Tell your class about one of the classmates you interviewed.**

Example:

I talked to James. He told me what he knows about the invention of flight. He knows that two brothers made the first airplane. The plane didn't stay in the air very long or fly very far, but it was an important flight. He couldn't remember exactly where they did it, but it was in the US.

✔ **Rate your own speaking**

Information:	OK	Good	Excellent
Fluency:	OK	Good	Excellent
Pronunciation:	OK	Good	Excellent

6 **Listen to each response and match it to the question it answers.** 🔊 **Track 30**

a. Why do you think the invention of the steam engine was important?

b. Imagine that TV had never been invented. How do you think that would change our lives?

c. Describe the most dangerous invention in the history of humankind.

•   • Response #1

•   • Response #2

•   • Response #3

For more practice, look at the transcripts on page 6 and practice these responses with a classmate.

7 **Choose one of the questions below. Prepare your own response to this question by writing notes in the provided space. Be sure to explain your answer.**

a. Why do you think the invention of the steam engine was important?

b. Imagine that TV had never been invented. How do you think that would change our lives?

c. Describe the most dangerous invention in the history of humankind.

Now share your response with a classmate.

Question: _____

My Notes

_____

_____

_____

_____

_____

✔ Rate your classmate's response:

Information:	OK	Good	Excellent
Fluency:	OK	Good	Excellent
Pronunciation:	OK	Good	Excellent

EXTRA PRACTICE

Try answering one or more of these questions for extra practice. Use at least three sentences in your response to each question.

1. How and why do people invent something new?
2. Why do you think the invention of the printing press was important?
3. How do you think the invention of computers changed our lives?
4. Do you think the fields of genetic engineering and cloning have a future? Explain.

Money

1 **Listen to the speakers. Check the type of answer the speaker gives.** 🔊 Track 31

a. Speaker #1: ☐ personal experience ☐ personal opinion

b. Speaker #2: ☐ personal experience ☐ personal opinion

c. Speaker #3: ☐ personal experience ☐ personal opinion

2 **Sort the words and phrases by writing them in the correct categories.**

property	odds	food	bets
clothing	taxes	blackjack	stocks
bonds	rent	poker	commodities

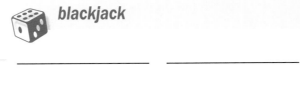

INVESTING

_____ _____

_____ _____

blackjack

_____ _____

_____ _____

EXPENSES

_____ _____

_____ _____

3 Listen to each dialog and read along. **Track 32**

 INVESTING

A: **Do you think it is wiser to save money in the bank or invest it?**

B: I think it is wiser to invest the money.

A: **How do you know what investment is best for you?**

B: If you do your homework before investing, you will be well aware of the risk associated with certain kinds of investments over others.

A: **What should you do with any extra money?**

B: Extra money should always be invested.

 GAMBLING

A: **Have you ever gambled?**

B: Yes, I sometimes like to gamble.

A: **Where have you gambled?**

B: I have been to a couple of casinos.

A: **Why can gambling be dangerous?**

B: Some people become so obsessed with winning that they gamble away everything that they have in the hope of winning their money back. That's dangerous.

EXPENSES

A: **What do you think you spend too much money on (e.g., clothes, shoes, entertainment, video games)?**

B: I think I spend too much money on food every day.

A: **How much do you usually spend?**

B: Every day, I buy a couple of drinks, some snacks, and lunch. By the end of the day, I spend ten dollars on food.

A: **Would you be willing to cut down on your spending?**

B: I want to cut down on this spending, but I am too lazy to prepare my lunch the night before I go to school.

Now practice these dialogs with a classmate.

4 **Choose one of the questions below. Prepare your answer to this question by writing notes below. Use the questions from Part 3 to help with your notes.**

a. Do you think it is wiser to save money in the bank or invest it?

b. Have you ever gambled?

c. What do you think you spend too much money on (e.g., clothes, shoes, entertainment, video games)?

Question: _____

My Notes

_____

_____

_____

Now interview two classmates. They will interview you as well. First, ask which question they chose. Then make notes of each answer.

My Classmates

Name: _____

Question: _____

_____

_____

_____

Name: _____

Question: _____

_____

_____

_____

5 **Tell your class about one of the classmates you interviewed.**

Example:

I talked to Karen. She told me that she had never gambled. She said that her parents taught her that gambling was a waste of time and money. Even though she doesn't live with her parents, she said that she isn't interested in gambling. She thinks it is silly.

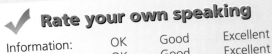

✔ **Rate your own speaking**

Information:	OK	Good	Excellent
Fluency:	OK	Good	Excellent
Pronunciation:	OK	Good	Excellent

6 **Listen to each response and match it to the question it answers.** 🔊 Track 33

a. Did you get an allowance when you were little? • • Response #1

b. If you had the choice, would you choose a job that brings satisfaction or a job that offers a good salary? Explain. • • Response #2

c. Explain the saying "Show me the money". • • Response #3

For more practice, look at the transcripts on page 6 and practice these responses with a classmate.

7 **Choose one of the questions below. Prepare your own response to this question by writing notes in the provided space. Be sure to explain your answer.**

a. Did you get an allowance when you were little?

b. If you had the choice, would you choose a job that brings satisfaction or a job that offers a good salary? Explain.

c. Explain the saying "Show me the money."

Now share your response with a classmate.

Question: _____

My Notes

_____

_____

_____

_____

_____

✔ Rate your classmate's response:

	OK	Good	Excellent
Information:	OK	Good	Excellent
Fluency:	OK	Good	Excellent
Pronunciation:	OK	Good	Excellent

Try answering one or more of these questions for extra practice. Use at least three sentences in your response to each question.

1. Explain the saying "Time is money."
2. Why do businesses often use the "buy now, pay later" approach?
3. If you won $1,000,000 in a lottery, what would you do with the money?
4. Where do people keep their money?

Parenting

1 **Listen to the speakers. Check the type of answer the speaker gives.** 🔊 Track 34

a. Speaker #1: ☐ personal experience ☐ personal opinion

b. Speaker #2: ☐ personal experience ☐ personal opinion

c. Speaker #3: ☐ personal experience ☐ personal opinion

2 **Sort the words and phrases by writing them in the correct categories.**

lots of love	tests	is unacceptable	encouragement
needs discipline	loses privileges	support	homework
schoolwork	classrooms	deserves grounding	care

EDUCATION

_____ _____

_____ _____

BAD BEHAVIOR

_____ _____

_____ _____

PARENTS AND CHILDREN

_____ _____

_____ _____

3 Listen to each dialog and read along. 🔊 Track 35

EDUCATION

A: How can parents teach their children the importance of education?

B: Parents can teach their kids the importance of education by setting a personal example and involving themselves in their children's learning.

A: What can they do?

B: If parents help their children with schoolwork, they show their kids that education is important.

A: What will happen if they do that?

B: Children will take their education more seriously and work harder.

BAD BEHAVIOR

A: Do you think parents should discipline their children for misbehavior and bad grades at school?

B: Yes, they should. There is no reason for parents to tolerate bad behavior or bad grades.

A: Should they use physical punishment?

B: I don't think they should use physical punishment.

A: What should they do instead of using physical punishment?

B: Instead, parents should temporarily take away privileges that the children enjoy.

PARENTS AND CHILDREN

A: Do you think children should support their parents when they get old?

B: Yes, of course.

A: Why should they support them?

B: Children should support their parents when they get old because their parents gave them life, love, support, and care for many years. Often, parents support their children in some way even after they have left home.

A: Is it normal in your culture for children to support their parents?

B: In my culture, many parents want to live independently from children when they are old, but children still need to provide support if parents need it.

Now practice these dialogs with a classmate.

4 **Choose one of the questions below. Prepare your answer to this question by writing notes below. Use the questions from Part 3 to help with your notes.**

a. How can parents teach their children the importance of education?

b. Do you think parents should discipline their children for misbehavior?

c. Do you think children should support their parents when they get old?

Question: _____

My Notes

_____

_____

_____

Now interview two classmates. They will interview you as well.
First, ask which question they chose. Then make notes of each answer.

My Classmates

Name: _____

Question: _____

_____

_____

_____

Name: _____

Question: _____

_____

_____

5 **Tell your class about one of the classmates you interviewed.**

Example:

I talked to Mike. He thinks that children should support their parents when the parents get old. He told me that he learned that from his parents. His grandfather lived with his family when he was growing up. Now Mike sees how important that was for both his grandfather and for his parents.

✓ **Rate your own speaking**

Information:	OK	Good	Excellent
Fluency:	OK	Good	Excellent
Pronunciation:	OK	Good	Excellent

6 Listen to each response and match it to the question it answers. 🔊 Track 36

a. How much time do you think parents should spend with their children? What should they do together?

• • Response #1

b. What valuable lessons can parents teach their children? Explain.

• • Response #2

c. Do you think parents should require their children to help with the household chores? Explain.

• • Response #3

For more practice, look at the transcripts on page 7 and practice these responses with a classmate.

7 Choose one of the questions below. Prepare your own response to this question by writing notes in the provided space. Be sure to explain your answer.

a. How much time do you think parents should spend with their children? What should they do together?

b. What valuable lessons can parents teach their children? Explain.

c. Do you think parents should require their children to help with the household chores? Explain.

Question: _____

My Notes

_____

_____

_____

_____

_____

Now share your response with a classmate.

✓ Rate your classmate's response:

Information:	OK	Good	Excellent
Fluency:	OK	Good	Excellent
Pronunciation:	OK	Good	Excellent

EXTRA PRACTICE

Try answering one or more of these questions for extra practice. Use at least three sentences in your response to each question.

1. Do you think parents should treat their sons and daughters equally? Explain.
2. When should children start making their own decisions about their lives?
3. What do you think grandparents can teach their grandchildren?
4. Recall one valuable lesson that your parents have taught you. Talk about it.

Space Exploration

1 **Listen to the speakers. Check the type of answer the speaker gives.** 🔊 Track 37

a. Speaker #1: ☐ personal experience ☐ personal opinion

b. Speaker #2: ☐ personal experience ☐ personal opinion

c. Speaker #3: ☐ personal experience ☐ personal opinion

2 **Sort the words and phrases by writing them in the correct categories.**

provides warmth	space stations	help us see faraway things
have lenses	gives us light	used by astronomers
space shuttles	space suits	far away from the Earth
range in size	space experiments	made of hydrogen and helium

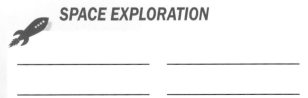

✴ **THE SUN**

_____ _____

_____ _____

🚀 **SPACE EXPLORATION**

_____ _____

_____ _____

🌙 **TELESCOPES**

_____ _____

_____ _____

3 **Listen to each dialog and read along.** ((•)) Track 38

☀ THE SUN

A: **What can you explain about the sun?**
B: The sun is a brightly burning mass of gases.
A: **What kinds of gas is the sun made of?**
B: It is mostly made of hydrogen and helium.
A: **What else do you know about it?**
B: Light that leaves the sun takes eight minutes to reach the Earth even though it is traveling at 300,000 kilometers per second.

 SPACE EXPLORATION

A: **What space stations or space shuttles do you know?**
B: I have heard about the space shuttles that were used by the US for space exploration.
A: **Where have you seen or learned about these things?**
B: I watched a couple of the space shuttle launches on television.
A: **What countries are currently exploring space?**
B: Currently many countries contribute to space exploration, including a joint venture by some countries in Europe.

☾ TELESCOPES

A: **What is a telescope used for?**
B: A telescope is a tool used to study star positions and movements.
A: **How big can telescopes get?**
B: Telescopes can range from very small ones to be used at home to very big ones to be used in a space observatory.
A: **What do you need for a really powerful telescope?**
B: For really powerful telescopes you need really big lenses. The size of the lens is what limits how powerful a telescope can be.

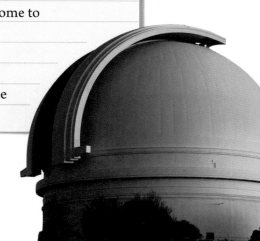

Now practice these dialogs with a classmate.

4 Choose one of the questions below. Prepare your answer to this question by writing notes below. Use the questions from Part 3 to help with your notes.

a. What can you explain about the sun?

b. What space stations/space shuttles do you know?

c. What is a telescope used for?

Question: _____

My Notes

_____

_____

_____

Now interview two classmates. They will interview you as well. First, ask which question they chose. Then make notes of each answer.

My Classmates

Name: _____

Question: _____

_____

_____

_____

Name: _____

Question: _____

_____

_____

_____

5 Tell your class about one of the classmates you interviewed.

Example:

I talked to Norma. She explained what she knows about the sun. The first thing she explained was the size of the sun. She said it is huge, much bigger than the Earth. She said the sun is like a big ball of fire, but it's much hotter than any fire we've ever seen.

✔ **Rate your own speaking**

Information:	OK	Good	Excellent
Fluency:	OK	Good	Excellent
Pronunciation:	OK	Good	Excellent

6 Listen to each response and match it to the question it answers. 🔊 Track 39

a. Do you believe that there are connections between star constellations and the predictions made in a horoscope? Explain. • • Response #1

b. Who was the first man in space? What do you know about him? • • Response #2

c. How did people try to study space in the past? • • Response #3

For more practice, look at the transcripts on page 8 and practice these responses with a classmate.

7 Choose one of the questions below. Prepare your own response to this question by writing notes in the provided space. Be sure to explain your answer.

Question: _____

My Notes

_____

_____

_____

_____

_____

a. Do you believe that there are connections between star constellations and the predictions made in a horoscope? Explain.

b. Who was the first man in space? What do you know about him?

c. How did people try to study space in the past?

Now share your response with a classmate.

Rate your classmate's response:

Information: OK   Good   Excellent
Fluency: OK   Good   Excellent
Pronunciation: OK   Good   Excellent

EXTRA PRACTICE

Try answering one or more of these questions for extra practice. Use at least three sentences in your response to each question.

1. Are horoscopes popular or important in your country? Explain.
2. What do you know about attempts to explore the moon?
3. Would you ever consider traveling into space?
4. Do you think there is life on other planets? Explain.

Superstitions

1 **Listen to the speakers. Check the type of answer the speaker gives.** 🔊 Track 40

a. Speaker #1: ☐ personal experience ☐ personal opinion

b. Speaker #2: ☐ personal experience ☐ personal opinion

c. Speaker #3: ☐ personal experience ☐ personal opinion

2 **Sort the words and phrases by writing them in the correct categories.**

belief in an unexplained power	a new penny	may have psychic powers
four-leaf clovers	use cards or tea leaves	spilling salt
faith-based	are sometimes con artists	a rabbit's foot
not based on reason	predict the future	not the same in all cultures

? **WHAT ARE SUPERSTITIONS**

_____ _____

_____ _____

☘ **SIGNS OF GOOD LUCK**

_____ _____

_____ _____

★ **FORTUNE TELLERS**

_____ _____

_____ _____

3 **Listen to each dialog and read along.** 🔊 Track 41

❓ SUPERSTITIONS

A: **What is a superstition?**

B: A superstition is a belief in the unexplained power of something or somebody that causes bad luck if you fail to observe it.

A: **Can you give an example of a superstition?**

B: For example, the number 13 is considered to be unlucky.

A: **Are you superstitious?**

B: I am not superstitious at all. I believe superstition is a product of ignorance.

🍀 SIGNS OF GOOD LUCK

A: **According to some people in your country, what brings good luck?**

B: According to some people in my country, finding a four-leaf clover or finding a new penny in the street will bring you good luck.

A: **Why are these items considered lucky charms?**

B: When I ask, nobody knows why these things are associated with good luck.

A: **Where do you think these good luck charms are from?**

B: They are very old superstitions handed down from generation to generation.

⭐ FORTUNE TELLERS

A: **Do you believe in fortune telling?**

B: No, I don't.

A: **Have you ever gone to a fortune-teller or a psychic?**

B: I have never gone to a fortune-teller in my life, but I did see how a person used her psychic powers to relieve my mother's headache.

A: **What did you think about that?**

B: It was amazing. My mom has tried everything, but that is the first time something took her headache away immediately.

Now practice these dialogs with a classmate.

4 **Choose one of the questions below. Prepare your answer to this question by writing notes below. Use the questions from Part 3 to help with your notes.**

a. What is a superstition?

b. According to some people in your country, what brings good luck?

c. Do you believe in fortune telling?

Question: _____

My Notes

_____

_____

_____

Now interview two classmates. They will interview you as well. First, ask which question they chose. Then make notes of each answer.

My Classmates

Name: _____

Question: _____

_____

_____

Name: _____

Question: _____

_____

_____

5 **Tell your class about one of the classmates you interviewed.**

Example:

I talked to Oliver. He told me about some things that people in his country think bring good luck. One funny thing that he talked about was a lucky kind of lizard. I'm not exactly sure what kind of lizard it is, but he said if people see one in their house, it's supposed to bring them luck.

✔ Rate your own speaking

Information:	OK	Good	Excellent
Fluency:	OK	Good	Excellent
Pronunciation:	OK	Good	Excellent

6 **Listen to each response and match it to the question it answers.** 🔊 **Track 42**

a. What are the lucky numbers in your country?   •   • Response #1

b. Do you believe black cats bring bad luck? Explain.   •   • Response #2

c. Do many people in your culture believe in horoscopes
and astrology? Explain.   •   • Response #3

**For more practice, look at the transcripts on page 8 and practice these responses with
a classmate.**

7 **Choose one of the questions below. Prepare your
own response to this question by writing notes in
the provided space. Be sure to explain your answer.**

a. What are the lucky numbers in your country?

b. Do you believe black cats bring bad luck? Explain.

c. Do many people in your culture believe in horoscopes
and astrology? Explain.

Question: _____

My Notes

_____

_____

_____

_____

_____

Now share your response with a classmate.

✔ Rate your classmate's response:

Information:	OK	Good	Excellent
Fluency:	OK	Good	Excellent
Pronunciation:	OK	Good	Excellent

EXTRA PRACTICE

**Try answering one or more of these questions for extra practice.
Use at least three sentences in your response to each question.**

1. Do you have lucky and unlucky numbers of your own? Explain.
2. Have you heard of any superstitions related to mirrors?
3. Do you believe in ghosts and spirits? Explain.
4. A superstition says if your right eye itches, you'll laugh soon. If your left eye itches,
you'll cry soon. Is there a similar superstition in your culture?

Television

1 Listen to the speakers. Check the type of answer the speaker gives. Track 43

a. Speaker #1: ☐ personal experience ☐ personal opinion

b. Speaker #2: ☐ personal experience ☐ personal opinion

c. Speaker #3: ☐ personal experience ☐ personal opinion

2 Sort the words and phrases by writing them in the correct categories.

high-definition	surround sound	supervise their children
plasma	flat-screen	audio input/output
guide children	block inappropriate shows	multiple speakers
explain a show's content	big-screen	digital sound technology

TYPES OF TELEVISIONS

_____ _____

_____ _____

 ADVANCED SOUND SYSTEMS

_____ _____

_____ _____

PARENTS' RESPONSIBILITIES

_____ _____

_____ _____

3 Listen to each dialog and read along. (⸜))) Track 44

 TYPES OF TELEVISIONS

A: **What kind of TV do you have?**
B: We have a huge plasma TV.
A: **How big is your plasma television?**
B: It is over fifty inches wide.
A: **What are the advantages of having this kind of TV?**
B: The advantages are that everything looks really clear. It's much better than on my small, old television.

♪ **ADVANCED SOUND SYSTEMS**

A: **What sound system do you have with your TV?**
B: We have a home-theater surround sound system that allows us to hear real-life sound effects.
A: **What real-life sound effects can you hear with your sound system?**
B: When I watch a movie, and someone opens a door, it is like a door is being opened right behind me.
A: **Why do you think home-theaters are so popular?**
B: They are popular because they create a life-like, rich sound that lets you enjoy the movie more fully.

PARENTS' RESPONSIBILITIES

A: **What do you think parents should do to make sure their children are not watching inappropriate programs?**
B: Parents should supervise and guide their children's TV viewing habits.
A: **What kinds of programming should parents stop their children from seeing?**
B: Parents shouldn't expose their children to anything that might frighten them or cause them to ask questions that they will not understand the answers to.
A: **Are adult-themed television shows fine for children?**
B: Shows with adult themes are certainly not OK for children to watch.

Now practice these dialogs with a classmate.

4 **Choose one of the questions below. Prepare your answer to this question by writing notes below. Use the questions from Part 3 to help with your notes.**

a. What kind of TV do you have (e.g., HDTV, plasma, flat-screen, big-screen)?

b. What sound system do you have with your TV?

c. How can parents make sure their children are not watching inappropriate programs?

Question: _____

My Notes

_____

_____

_____

Now interview two classmates. They will interview you as well. First, ask which question they chose. Then make notes of each answer.

My Classmates

Name: _____

Question: _____

_____

_____

_____

Name: _____

Question: _____

_____

_____

_____

5 **Tell your class about one of the classmates you interviewed.**

Example:

I talked to Paula. She explained what parents need to do to make sure their children aren't watching inappropriate programs on TV. The main thing she talked about was direct supervision. By that, she means that the parents need to be watching TV with their kids.

✔ **Rate your own speaking**

Information:	OK	Good	Excellent
Fluency:	OK	Good	Excellent
Pronunciation:	OK	Good	Excellent

6 **Listen to each response and match it to the question it answers.** 🔊 Track 45

a. What TV channels can you watch on your TV? Which one is your favorite? Why?

b. How much time do you think people should spend watching TV? Explain.

c. Describe how you think life would be without a TV.

• • Response #1

• • Response #2

• • Response #3

For more practice, look at the transcripts on page 9 and practice these responses with a classmate.

7 **Choose one of the questions below. Prepare your own response to this question by writing notes in the provided space. Be sure to explain your answer.**

a. What TV channels can you watch on your TV? Which one is your favorite? Why?

b. How much time do you think people should spend watching TV? Explain.

c. Describe how you think life would be without a TV.

Now share your response with a classmate.

Question: _____

My Notes

_____

_____

_____

_____

_____

✔ Rate your classmate's response:

	OK	Good	Excellent
Information:	OK	Good	Excellent
Fluency:	OK	Good	Excellent
Pronunciation:	OK	Good	Excellent

EXTRA PRACTICE

Try answering one or more of these questions for extra practice. Use at least three sentences in your response to each question.

1. Do you think people are becoming lazier because of TV? Explain.
2. Do you think there are too many commercials on TV? Explain.
3. Should commercials be prohibited on kids' channels? Why or why not?
4. Should TV programs be rated? Why or why not?

Stress

.... ❶ **Listen to the speakers. Check the type of answer the speaker gives.** 🔊 Track 46

    a. Speaker #1: ☐ personal experience   ☐ personal opinion

    b. Speaker #2: ☐ personal experience   ☐ personal opinion

    c. Speaker #3: ☐ personal experience   ☐ personal opinion

.... ❷ **Sort the words and phrases by writing them in the correct categories.**

can't sleep	supporting a family	working efficiently
not procrastinating	can't relax	meeting deadlines
raising children	paying bills	can be caused by stress
bad for your health	using time wisely	saving for the future

💡 **ADULT RESPONSIBILITIES**

_____   _____

_____   _____

🌙 **INSOMNIA**

_____   _____

_____   _____

🕐 **TIME MANAGEMENT**

_____   _____

_____   _____

3 Listen to each dialog and read along. Track 47

ADULT RESPONSIBILITIES

A: **What do you think are the main causes of stress?**

B: The main cause of stress is the buildup of responsibility as people get older.

A: **What are you responsible for when you are young?**

B: When you are young, you are not responsible for anything.

A: **What happens when you get older?**

B: As you get older, you have to work hard to earn money for food, then to pay for a place to live.

INSOMNIA

A: **Why do you think some people have insomnia when they are under stress?**

B: When people are under stress, they can't sleep because they can't unwind and stop thinking about their problems.

A: **Does stress only affect a person physically?**

B: Stress can affect you both physically and mentally.

A: **Explain how stress keeps a person awake.**

B: When you keep worrying about a problem, your mind can't relax. If your brain isn't relaxed, your body can't relax either.

TIME MANAGEMENT

A: **How can proper time management reduce stress?**

B: Proper time management reduces stress by helping people stay on top of jobs or requests given to them by others.

A: **Who is normally stressed?**

B: People who have demanding jobs with constant deadlines can become repeatedly stressed.

A: **How does working efficiently reduce stress?**

B: Working efficiently allows you to reach your deadlines on time, and this reduces stress.

Now practice these dialogs with a classmate.

4 **Choose one of the questions below. Prepare your answer to this question by writing notes below. Use the questions from Part 3 to help with your notes.**

a. What do you think are the main causes of stress?

b. Why do you think some people have insomnia when they are under stress?

c. How can proper time management reduce stress?

Question: _____

My Notes

_____

_____

_____

Now interview two classmates. They will interview you as well. First, ask which question they chose. Then make notes of each answer.

My Classmates

Name: _____

Question: _____

_____

_____

_____

Name: _____

Question: _____

_____

_____

_____

5 **Tell your class about one of the classmates you interviewed.**

Example:

I talked to Ryan. He told me some of the main causes of stress in his life. Of course, the main cause of stress for Ryan is studying. He has to get good grades so that he can keep his scholarship. That gives him a lot of stress. In fact, next week he has two big tests, so he's really stressed out right now.

Rate your own speaking

Information:	OK	Good	Excellent
Fluency:	OK	Good	Excellent
Pronunciation:	OK	Good	Excellent

6 Listen to each response and match it to the question it answers. 🔊 Track 48

a. Do you discuss your stressful situations with your friends? Explain.

b. How do you relax in your free time?

c. What would you choose: a very stressful job with a high salary or an easy job with low pay? Explain.

• • Response #1

• • Response #2

• • Response #3

For more practice, look at the transcripts on page 9 and practice these responses with a classmate.

7 Choose one of the questions below. Prepare your own response to this question by writing notes in the provided space. Be sure to explain your answer.

a. Do you discuss stressful situations with your friends? Explain.

b. How do you relax in your free time?

c. What would you choose: a very stressful job with a high salary or an easy job with low pay? Explain.

Now share your response with a classmate.

Question: _____

My Notes

_____
_____
_____
_____
_____

Rate your classmate's response:

	OK	Good	Excellent
Information:	OK	Good	Excellent
Fluency:	OK	Good	Excellent
Pronunciation:	OK	Good	Excellent

EXTRA PRACTICE

Try answering one or more of these questions for extra practice. Use at least three sentences in your response to each question.

1. How do you deal with school-related stress?
2. Why do you think some people gain weight when they are under stress?
3. Describe a stressful situation that you have been in.
4. How can setting realistic goals reduce stress? Explain.

Memories

1 **Listen to the speakers. Check the type of answer the speaker gives.** 🔊 Track 49

a. Speaker #1:   ☐ personal experience   ☐ personal opinion

b. Speaker #2:   ☐ personal experience   ☐ personal opinion

c. Speaker #3:   ☐ personal experience   ☐ personal opinion

2 **Sort the words and phrases by writing them in the correct categories.**

are buddies	book exercises	scary decorations	lessons
know each other	talk closely	practice tests	dress up
receive candy	play together	trick-or-treating	assignments

 BEST FRIENDS

_____   _____

_____   _____

🎓 **LEARNING**

_____   _____

_____   _____

🎃 **HALLOWEEN**

_____   _____

_____   _____

3 **Listen to each dialog and read along.** 🔊 Track 50

BEST FRIENDS

A: **Do you remember your best friend from childhood?**

B: Yes, I do. I remember my childhood friend very well.

A: **What did you do together?**

B: We usually played together in my friend's front yard.

A: **Describe him or her.**

B: She was much more confident than I was, and she was very athletic.

LEARNING

A: **Do you remember how you began studying English?**

B: My sister is eight years older than me, and so she started learning English long before me. She taught me my first words in English.

A: **Why did you want to do that?**

B: I wanted to be like her so badly that I would sit next to her when she would do her English homework.

A: **How did that help you later?**

B: Eventually, when I started learning English, it was much easier for me because I had been studying with my sister for all that time.

HALLOWEEN

A: **What was your favorite holiday when you were a child?**

B: When I was little, I loved to celebrate Halloween.

A: **Did you go trick-or-treating?**

B: On Halloween evening, we would go out trick-or-treating with my dad.

A: **What happened when you got older?**

B: As my brothers and I got older, my mom didn't decorate the house as much. By the time we got to high school, we barely celebrated Halloween at all.

Now practice these dialogs with a classmate.

4 **Choose one of the questions below. Prepare your answer to this question by writing notes below. Use the questions from Part 3 to help with your notes.**

a. Do you remember your best friend from childhood?

b. Do you remember how you began studying English?

c. What was your favorite holiday when you were a child?

Question: _____

My Notes

_____

_____

_____

Now interview two classmates. They will interview you as well. First, ask which question they chose. Then make notes of each answer.

My Classmates

Name: _____

Question: _____

_____

_____

_____

Name: _____

Question: _____

_____

_____

5 **Tell your class about one of the classmates you interviewed.**

Example:

I talked to Sonia. She talked about her first English class. She said that she took that class when she was in middle school. There were lots of students in the class, so they didn't really study speaking or writing. She said they mostly studied grammar, and she didn't like it.

Rate your own speaking

	OK	Good	Excellent
Information:	OK	Good	Excellent
Fluency:	OK	Good	Excellent
Pronunciation:	OK	Good	Excellent

6   **Listen to each response and match it to the question it answers.** 🔊 **Track 51**

a. Describe an unpleasant event that you remember. •   • Response #1

b. Talk about a school teacher whom you remember well. •   • Response #2

c. Describe your favorite photograph. •   • Response #3

For more practice, look at the transcripts on page 10 and practice these responses with a classmate.

7   **Choose one of the questions below. Prepare your own response to this question by writing notes in the provided space. Be sure to explain your answer.**

a. Describe an unpleasant event that you remember.

b. Talk about a school teacher whom you remember well.

c. Describe your favorite photograph.

Now share your response with a classmate.

Question: _____

My Notes

_____

_____

_____

_____

_____

Rate your classmate's response:

Information:	OK	Good	Excellent
Fluency:	OK	Good	Excellent
Pronunciation:	OK	Good	Excellent

EXTRA PRACTICE

Try answering one or more of these questions for extra practice. Use at least three sentences in your response to each question.

1. Describe something you remember about one of your grandparents.
2. What do you remember about yourself as a teenager?
3. How well can you recall people's faces and/or names?
4. Talk about one thing you would like to forget.

Phobias

1 **Listen to the speakers. Check the type of answer the speaker gives.** 🔊 Track 52

a. Speaker #1: ☐ personal experience   ☐ personal opinion

b. Speaker #2: ☐ personal experience   ☐ personal opinion

c. Speaker #3: ☐ personal experience   ☐ personal opinion

2 **Sort the words and phrases by writing them in the correct categories.**

afraid	parachuting	sharks	spiders
bungee jumping	snakes	nervous	calm
skateboarding	fish	scared	bicycle racing

DIFFERENT EMOTIONS

_____   _____

_____   _____

EXTREME SPORTS

_____   _____

_____   _____

CREEPY CREATURES

_____   _____

_____   _____

3 **Listen to each dialog and read along.** 🔊 Track 53

 DIFFERENT EMOTIONS

A: **Is there anything that makes you nervous or afraid?**

B: I am afraid of spiders. This is called arachnophobia.

A: **Do you see them a lot?**

B: Unfortunately, I live in Australia where there are many large and sometimes poisonous spiders.

A: **Where do you see them?**

B: Often they come into my house, and I find them in the kitchen sink or in the bathtub.

 **EXTREME SPORTS**

A: **Would you consider participating in extreme sports?**

B: Of course! I have done a solo parachute jump from 1000 meters and four bungee jumps from about 150 meters.

A: **Have you tried any others?**

B: I also did a canyon swing, which is a huge jump followed by swinging on a 200 meter long rope.

A: **Why do you enjoy it so much?**

B: I love the adrenalin rush you get from these sports.

 CREEPY CREATURES

A: **What dangers do you face when you go swimming in the ocean?**

B: In the ocean, there are marine creatures that might attack people as they swim.

A: **How do you know that? What makes you think that?**

B: I've always thought that ever since I watched a movie about a giant shark that attacked people while they were swimming.

A: **Were you afraid to go swimming in the ocean after you saw that movie?**

B: I was afraid to go in the ocean for three months after that.

Now practice these dialogs with a classmate.

4 Choose one of the questions below. Prepare your answer to this question by writing notes below. Use the questions from Part 3 to help with your notes.

a. Is there anything that makes you nervous or afraid?

b. Would you consider participating in extreme sports?

c. What dangers do you face when you go swimming in the ocean?

Question: _____

My Notes

_____

_____

_____

Now interview two classmates. They will interview you as well. First, ask which question they chose. Then make notes of each answer.

My Classmates

Name: _____

Question: _____

_____

_____

_____

Name: _____

Question: _____

_____

_____

5 Tell your class about one of the classmates you interviewed.

Example:

I talked to Thomas. He told me about the danger of rip tides for people swimming in the ocean. I was surprised that he didn't talk about fish or dangerous sea animals, but Thomas pointed out that a lot of people drown because of rip tides.

✔ **Rate your own speaking**

Information:	OK	Good	Excellent
Fluency:	OK	Good	Excellent
Pronunciation:	OK	Good	Excellent

6 Listen to each response and match it to the question it answers. Track 54

a. Why do you think many people are afraid of going to the dentist? Are you? Explain.

Response #1

b. Why are some people afraid of dogs? Have you had a negative experience with dogs? Explain.

Response #2

c. What were you afraid of when you were little? Why?

Response #3

For more practice, look at the transcripts on page 10 and practice these responses with a classmate.

7 Choose one of the questions below. Prepare your own response to this question by writing notes in the provided space. Be sure to explain your answer.

a. Why do you think many people are afraid of going to the dentist? Are you? Explain.

b. Why are some people afraid of dogs? Have you had a negative experience with dogs? Explain.

c. What were you afraid of when you were little? Why?

Now share your response with a classmate.

Question: _____

My Notes

_____

_____

_____

_____

_____

Rate your classmate's response:

	OK	Good	Excellent
Information:	OK	Good	Excellent
Fluency:	OK	Good	Excellent
Pronunciation:	OK	Good	Excellent

EXTRA PRACTICE

Try answering one or more of these questions for extra practice. Use at least three sentences in your response to each question.

1. Do you like watching scary movies? Explain.
2. Do you celebrate Halloween or a similar holiday in your country? Explain.
3. Give examples of phobias that you know.
4. How do you think people overcome their fears?

Social Issues

1 **Listen to the speakers. Check the type of answer the speaker gives.** Track 55

a. Speaker #1: ☐ personal experience ☐ personal opinion

b. Speaker #2: ☐ personal experience ☐ personal opinion

c. Speaker #3: ☐ personal experience ☐ personal opinion

2 **Sort the words and phrases by writing them in the correct categories.**

poverty	subsidized housing	can't always buy food
daycare facilities	unemployment rates	find it hard to pay rent
crime rates	homelessness	national healthcare
public schooling	have a poorer quality of life	can't afford medication

SOCIAL PROBLEMS

_____ _____

_____ _____

LOWER INCOME FAMILIES

_____ _____

_____ _____

GOVERNMENT PROGRAMS

_____ _____

_____ _____

3 **Listen to each dialog and read along.** 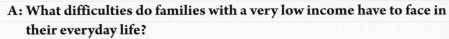 Track 56

SOCIAL PROBLEMS

A: **Describe common problems that any society has to deal with.**

B: I think the most common problems are poverty, unemployment, caring for the homeless, and crime.

A: **Which should be fixed first?**

B: Poverty is particularly important because it includes and can lead to all the others.

A: **Can you give some examples?**

B: Poverty can lead to drug abuse which in turn can lead to crime and homelessness.

LOWER INCOME FAMILIES

A: **What difficulties do families with a very low income have to face in their everyday life?**

B: They have to feed and clothe their children, pay rent, purchase medication, and get other basic necessities on a daily basis.

A: **Which is the most important?**

B: Making sure that families have a place to live and food to eat are the most important things.

A: **Why is it so important to deal with this problem?**

B: People can die without food or shelter.

GOVERNMENT PROGRAMS

A: **What government programs do you have in your country to help disadvantaged families with young children?**

B: Government programs include heavily subsidizing families with low incomes.

A: **Are there any others?**

B: My government also provides daycare facilities for families who cannot afford to send young children anywhere while they work.

A: **Can you think of an example of a program for children?**

B: I have seen centers for older children, to educate them further after school and keep them occupied.

Now practice these dialogs with a classmate.

4 **Choose one of the questions below. Prepare your answer to this question by writing notes below. Use the questions from Part 3 to help with your notes.**

a. Describe common problems that any society has to deal with.

b. What difficulties do families with very low incomes have to face in their everyday life?

c. What government programs do you have in your country to help disadvantaged families with young children?

Question: _____

My Notes

_____

_____

_____

**Now interview two classmates. They will interview you as well.
First, ask which question they chose. Then make notes of each answer.**

My Classmates

Name: _____

Question: _____

_____

_____

_____

Name: _____

Question: _____

_____

_____

_____

5 **Tell your class about one of the classmates you interviewed.**

Example:

I talked to Vera. She explained two common social problems, which are poverty and crime. In her opinion, a society can lower the crime rate if they first lower the poverty rate. She strongly believes that poverty and crime are related problems.

✔ **Rate your own speaking**

Information:	OK	Good	Excellent
Fluency:	OK	Good	Excellent
Pronunciation:	OK	Good	Excellent

6 **Listen to each response and match it to the question it answers.** 🔊 Track 57

a. What do you think the government needs to do to make sure that fewer families fall below the poverty line? • • Response #1

b. What do you think of the quality of health care in your country? Explain. • • Response #2

c. What do you think of the crime rates in your country? Explain. • • Response #3

For more practice, look at the transcripts onpage 11 and practice these responses with a classmate.

7 **Choose one of the questions below. Prepare your own response to this question by writing notes in the provided space. Be sure to explain your answer.**

a. What do you think the government needs to do to make sure that fewer families fall below the poverty line?

b. What do you think of the quality of health care in your country? Explain.

c. What do you think of the crime rates in your country? Explain.

Now share your response with a classmate.

Question: _____

My Notes

_____
_____
_____
_____
_____

✔ Rate your classmate's response:

	OK	Good	Excellent
Information:	OK	Good	Excellent
Fluency:	OK	Good	Excellent
Pronunciation:	OK	Good	Excellent

EXTRA PRACTICE

Try answering one or more of these questions for extra practice. Use at least three sentences in your response to each question.

1. What needs to be done to take care of homeless children?
2. What do you think of medical insurance options in your country?
3. What is the level of unemployment in your country?
4. Describe any problems with drugs and drug trafficking in your country.

Media and News

1 **Listen to the speakers. Check the type of answer the speaker gives.** 🔊 Track 58

a. Speaker #1: ☐ personal experience   ☐ personal opinion

b. Speaker #2: ☐ personal experience   ☐ personal opinion

c. Speaker #3: ☐ personal experience   ☐ personal opinion

2 **Sort the words and phrases by writing them in the correct categories.**

front page	magazine ads	spy with cameras	sports section
radio spots	follow celebrities	TV commercials	don't respect privacy
Internet campaigns	want hot news	business section	entertainment section

📰 PARTS OF A NEWSPAPER

_____   _____

_____   _____

📊 HOW BUSINESSES USE MASS MEDIA

_____   _____

_____   _____

⭐ PAPARAZZI

_____   _____

_____   _____

3 **Listen to each dialog and read along.** 🔊 Track 59

PARTS OF A NEWSPAPER

A: What sections of a newspaper do you prefer to read the most?

B: I like to read the front-page articles of every section in the newspaper.

A: Why do you prefer to read those?

B: By reading the front pages, I get a great idea of what is happening without having to devote a lot of time to the newspaper.

A: Is that all that you read in the newspaper?

B: Sometimes I look at the editorial section as well, but not always.

HOW BUSINESSES USE MASS MEDIA

A: How do newspapers and magazines help with business?

B: Newspapers and magazines can help promote businesses because they print advertisements and reviews that can help attract customers.

A: How many people do they reach?

B: Newspapers are read every day by millions of people.

A: Why do businesses advertise in newspapers?

B: If businesses want to announce plans or just tell people that they exist, they can use the newspaper to gain exposure that would be difficult to get otherwise.

⭐ PAPARAZZI

A: Sometimes, when paparazzi try to acquire hot news about celebrities, they violate celebrities' privacy and can even put celebrities' lives in danger. What do you think about how paparazzi get news?

B: I think that the ways in which paparazzi sometimes get news are really immoral.

A: What techniques do they use to get their stories?

B: They spy with their cameras by celebrities' houses and clubs trying to get a "sensational" shot that would get them a big paycheck.

A: What should the paparazzi do instead of using these methods?

B: They should respect the boundaries of people's personal and professional lives.

Now practice these dialogs with a classmate.

4 **Choose one of the questions below. Prepare your answer to this question by writing notes below. Use the questions from Part 3 to help with your notes.**

a. What sections of a newspaper do you prefer to read the most?

b. How do newspapers and magazines help with business?

c. What do you think about how paparazzi get news?

Question: _____

My Notes

_____

_____

_____

Now interview two classmates. They will interview you as well. First, ask which question they chose. Then make notes of each answer.

My Classmates

Name: _____

Question: _____

_____

_____

_____

Name: _____

Question: _____

_____

_____

5 **Tell your class about one of the classmates you interviewed.**

Example:

I talked to Walter. He thinks that newspapers and magazines mainly help businesses advertise their products. Businesses know that newspaper or magazine ads can help them sell more products and increase their profits.

Rate your own speaking

	OK	Good	Excellent
Information:	OK	Good	Excellent
Fluency:	OK	Good	Excellent
Pronunciation:	OK	Good	Excellent

6 Listen to each response and match it to the question it answers. 🔊 **Track 60**

a. How do you think mass media influence our opinions about news events?

b. What is news? Explain.

c. Talk about the latest issues in foreign news.

•   • Response #1

•   • Response #2

•   • Response #3

For more practice, look at the transcripts on page 11 and practice these responses with a classmate.

7 Choose one of the questions below. Prepare your own response to this question by writing notes in the provided space. Be sure to explain your answer.

a. How do you think mass media influence our opinions about news events?

b. What is news? Explain.

c. Talk about the latest issues in foreign news.

Now share your response with a classmate.

Question: _____

My Notes
_____
_____
_____
_____
_____

✔ **Rate your classmate's response:**

Information:	OK	Good	Excellent
Fluency:	OK	Good	Excellent
Pronunciation:	OK	Good	Excellent

EXTRA PRACTICE

Try answering one or more of these questions for extra practice. Use at least three sentences in your response to each question.

1. What kinds of news do you like to watch on TV?
2. What are the most popular newspapers in your country?
3. How is listening to news on the radio important for our everyday lives?
4. What is "yellow press" and why is it popular?

Just Speak Up

Olga Geissler

Transcripts

Answer Key

3

Unit 01 Meeting People

Track 1

❶ **Listen to the speakers. Check the type of answer the speaker gives.**

a. Speaker #1: If I could be some kind of animal, I think I'd want to be a dog. They always look like they're having fun. I wouldn't want to be a wild dog, though. I would want to be a dog that someone keeps in their house.

b. Speaker #2: My most precious possession is a necklace that my parents gave me for my birthday. I got the necklace when I was six years old. My mother gave me the necklace on my first day of school. It has a picture of my mother and father in it. It's not a valuable necklace, but it's very precious to me.

c. Speaker #3: I think it's important for friends to have similar interests. If they don't have any similar interests, what can they do when they get together? They don't have anything to talk about or to do. On the other hand, if two people like some of the same things, then they can enjoy those things when they spend time with each other.

Track 3

❻ **Listen to each response and match it to the question it answers.**

Response #1: Because a good friend is like my sibling, it is important for me to be able to trust my friend unconditionally. I should be able to rely on her help at any time and to know that she can just listen to me when I need it. But a good friend should also be able to tell me to stop complaining if I am being silly.

Response #2: If I were not in class, I would be outside in the sun. I live in Sydney, and I enjoy spending time at the beach or playing football with my friends in the local park. There are more than thirty beaches in Sydney, and so far I've seen more than half of them.

Response #3: No, I wouldn't because famous people have no privacy. They are under constant scrutiny and can't go anywhere without paparazzi following them. In fact, Princess Diana died in a car accident trying to escape from the press in a high-speed chase.

Unit 02 Sports

Track 4

❶ **Listen to the speakers. Check the type of answer the speaker gives.**

a. Speaker #1: I used to play on my school's basketball team when I was younger. After I started high school, I didn't have much free time, so I had to quit playing. I enjoyed being on the team. Sometimes we would travel to other cities for games.

b. Speaker #2: My favorite soccer player is David Beckham. He is from England, but now he plays for a soccer team in the US. He is probably one of the greatest soccer players of all time. A lot of people also think that he is really good looking.

c. Speaker #3: The last sports event that I watched in a stadium was a baseball game. I went there with my family. My father got free tickets from the office where he works, so that is why we could go. The seats were pretty good, and I really enjoyed the game. The weather was nice that day, too.

Track 6

❻ **Listen to each response and match it to the question it answers.**

Response #1: I enjoy watching rugby. I get really excited about supporting my country's team in the rugby world cup. My country has one of the best teams in the world. We often get to the semifinals only to be beaten by New Zealand or Australia. I also enjoy watching because I play rugby, and know how it feels.

Response #2: : I think women should play any sport men play. To say otherwise is discrimination. Though women are not as strong as men, they can easily compete in the same sports against other women. As long as women are not using the same

1

equipment as men, for example in weight lifting, they should be encouraged to compete in all kinds of sports.

Response #3: Injuries are the worst thing that can happen to professional athletes because they can finish the athletes' careers and lives. For example, when a tennis player injures his elbow, he can't play anymore. Many players continue in the world of sport by becoming coaches or commentators, often for the TV, radio, or newspapers.

Unit 03 Friendship

Track 7

❶ **Listen to the speakers. Check the type of answer the speaker gives.**

a. Speaker #1: My definition of a friend is someone whom you know something about. You can't really say someone is your friend if you just know their name and their face. But if you spend time together and get to know each other well, then you can call that person your friend.

b. Speaker #2: One thing you should never do is give your friend a lot of money. That is a sure way to ruin a friendship. If you give your friend a lot of money, then you start worrying about when you will get the money back. It also makes your friend worry about how to pay you back.

c. Speaker #3: The last time that I helped a friend was a few days ago. I didn't do much. I just went out to a coffee shop with my friend and listened to his problems. He needed someone to talk to. That was how I helped him.

Track 9

❻ **Listen to each response and match it to the question it answers.**

Response #1: Friends can often pressure people into doing things that they do not normally do. This can lead to negative consequences. Many children start smoking because they see their friends doing it and they want to fit in.

Response #2: The saying, "Tell me who your friends are, and I will tell you who you are," means that people judge you by your friends, people you associate with. This is due to the fact that friends tend to value the same things and act in a certain way. If your friends value something like humor, then more than likely, you will be funny yourself.

Response #3: While it is more difficult, it is possible to be friends with older people. People with similar interests will always want to be friends with each other. If a grandfather and a child both like baseball, they instantly have something that they can start a friendship around.

Unit 04 Holidays

Track 10

❶ **Listen to the speakers. Check the type of answer the speaker gives.**

a. Speaker #1: I live in an apartment, so there isn't much decorating we can do for the holidays. I guess one thing we do in my family is decorate our door. My mother has a special wreath of flowers that she puts on our door during the holiday season.

b. Speaker #2: Independence Day in my country is during the summer. On that day last summer, I ate hamburgers in my friend's backyard. His father cooked the hamburgers on their outdoor grill. Then, after it was dark, we went to see some fireworks.

c. Speaker #3: My favorite holiday is Labor Day. I know that sounds strange, but for me, it's a great holiday. We always have a three-day weekend for Labor Day, which gives everyone extra time to relax. Other holidays might fall on a weekend, so then everyone gets less time off!

Track 12

❻ **Listen to each response and match it to the question it answers.**

Response #1: My country celebrates many holidays from many different religions and parts of the world. But I think that the most significant holiday

is Thanksgiving. It is so important because it is the one holiday that people of every background can celebrate. It celebrates the appreciation of everything that you are grateful for in your life.

Response #2: My family has a tradition of cooking scrambled eggs in a special way for the holidays. To make this dish, we take crackers and break them into the eggs. Then we scramble the eggs and sometimes cover the eggs in strawberry jam. It is delicious.

Response #3: When I was little we would always celebrate the Jewish holiday of Yom Kippur. We had to go an entire day without eating or drinking as a part of that special day. I always remember around 4 or 5 o'clock watching my mom prepare dinner for that night, and feeling my stomach growl.

Unit 05 Stereotypes

Track 13

❶ **Listen to the speakers. Check the type of answer the speaker gives.**

a. Speaker #1: A typical man's role in the family is to make money. Most fathers spend five or six days a week outside the home working at their jobs. They leave early and come home late, so they can't help out much around the house or with kids. Their role is just to provide income for the household.

b. Speaker #2: My brother was always concerned about his body image. He tried lots of different kinds of diets and he did various kinds of exercises to shape his body. He wanted a flat stomach and big arm muscles. These days, he is too busy studying, so he can't do all that stuff anymore.

c. Speaker #3: When I was growing up, there wasn't a difference between the chores I had to do and the chores my sisters had to do. We all had to clean our rooms, wash dishes, do the laundry, and take care of things around the house. My sisters even had to mow the lawn. Usually people think that is a guy's job, but not in my family!

Track 15

❻ **Listen to each response and match it to the question it answers.**

Response #1: I think a father can raise his daughter alone, but it would be extremely difficult for him and his daughter. Only a woman can truly understand other women and all of the things that they go through. He might find it especially difficult to communicate with her and understand her during her teenage years.

Response #2: In my culture, it has traditionally been the role of the mother to take care of the children. Now, things are starting to change. Men and women now often share the responsibility of raising children. This is due to the fact that both men and women are now often busy with their careers.

Response #3: In my culture, many sports are open for participation from both men and women. The biggest exception to this is American football. American football is seen as very violent. Women's leagues are not so common due to the rough-and-tumble nature of the sport.

Unit 06 Time Management

Track 16

❶ **Listen to the speakers. Check the type of answer the speaker gives.**

a. Speaker #1: I spend a lot of my free time reading. Last weekend, I didn't have any plans, so I just stayed home and read a book. I got a new mystery novel by an author that I really like, and I finished the whole thing in one day! I guess I read for about five hours that day.

b. Speaker #2: In order not to forget important dates or appointments, I write things down. I write notes on little pieces of colored paper, and I stick these notes on my computer. Then, whenever I work on my computer, I see these notes and remember those dates and times.

c. Speaker #3: Kids in school these days seem busier than kids in the past. There seems to be a lot more school work and studying required now. In the past, kids had more free time to have fun with their friends. Now, it's just study, study, study all the time.

Track 18

⑥ **Listen to each response and match it to the question it answers.**

Response #1: I am a high school student, and I spend about 8 hours a day at school. I don't think it is too much because I know how important it is to get a good education. I also get to see all my friends at high school every day, so I am not unhappy spending so much time there.

Response #2: I spend a lot of time browsing the Internet. When I do research for my assignments, I find it easiest to get the information online. When I am finished with assignments, I still stay online. I don't think it is too much because there are so many cool things to do online, including playing games, listening to music, and looking at pictures of places I want to visit when I am older.

Response #3: It's important to manage your time wisely because you don't want to find yourself in a situation when you have to complete a month's worth of work in one week. It's very stressful and lowers the quality of your work. It also takes away from the time you should be relaxing or having fun.

Unit 07   Schooling

Track 19

① **Listen to the speakers. Check the type of answer the speaker gives.**

a. Speaker #1: Homeschooling has a couple of interesting advantages, I think. For one thing, kids get to spend more quality time with their parents when they are homeschooled. That extra time can have lots of benefits for a child. I think kids can also finish their work a lot faster when they are

homeschooled. A lot of time in public school is wasted on stuff other than just studying.

b. Speaker #2: I have never taken a class that used a computer more than a textbook. In one of my classes last semester, we had to do some work in the computer lab, but we still studied most of the material for the class out of a textbook. The teacher gave us lectures and we had reading assignments most of the time. We only went to the computer lab once a week.

c. Speaker #3: Taking an online class is not as good as taking the same class in a regular classroom. For one thing, if you're watching an online lecture at home on your computer, there are lots of distractions. Those can keep you from paying close attention. It's also harder to ask the teacher any questions during an online class. You can't just raise your hand to ask something during the lecture.

Track 21

⑥ **Listen to each response and match it to the question it answers.**

Response #1: Homeschooled children often find it harder to learn certain social skills. As a result, they might find it harder to work in groups, or be part of a team when they get older. The schooling process teaches kids how to interact with others, and this part is often difficult to reproduce in the home-schooled environment.

Response #2: Student-teacher interactions have many positive and negative results. Teachers have a tremendous amount of influence when it comes to a child's interest in a subject. If a teacher connects with a student, it can create a positive life-long passion for the subject. However, if the interaction is negative, the teacher can turn the student off of the subject forever.

Response #3: The disadvantages of public schooling are the inability to study at your own pace and your own time. Also it is necessary to deal with peer pressure and issues with teachers and administrators. Many quiet children often get overlooked and ignored in public school due to the sheer number of students that teachers need to care for.

Unit 08 Politics

Track 22

1 **Listen to the speakers. Check the type of answer the speaker gives.**

a. Speaker #1: I did not have a chance to vote in the last election in my country. I was too young at that time. I remember watching television on the night of the election with my parents. My father was disappointed because the candidate he voted for didn't win.

b. Speaker #2: The best form of government is a democracy. In this kind of government, the people can vote and they can have some influence in how the country is run. The power of government officials is spread out, so one person can't control the whole country.

c. Speaker #3: The court system of my country seems fair to me. Anyone who has to go to court gets to have a lawyer. If he or she can't afford a lawyer, then the government helps pay for a lawyer. Cases are also heard by juries in my country. The jury decides if a person is really guilty or not.

Track 24

6 **Listen to each response and match it to the question it answers.**

Response #1: The leader of my country is called the "Taoiseach". This means first minister. He is the head of the democratically voted government of the country. If his party has a majority in government, they can vote in new legislation, though any change in the constitution must be voted on by the whole country.

Response #2: The office of president is voted on every seven years in my country. However, the president does not have any serious political powers. Every four years, local elections are carried out to vote in ministers for each constituency. These ministers, organized into parties, ultimately determine the legislation in my country.

Response #3: Yes, the last two presidents in my country were women. However, the president in my country is more of a figurehead as he or she doesn't really have any major political power. He or she acts more as a representative to other countries by visiting areas in need of financial aid. The president highlights problems, such as poverty in developing countries.

Unit 09 If You Could

Track 25

1 **Listen to the speakers. Check the type of answer the speaker gives.**

a. Speaker #1: If I got a chance, I would like to visit the Great Pyramids in Egypt. I've seen so many pictures of the pyramids. I think it would be awesome to see them up close and in person. It would be a great experience to visit such a historical place.

b. Speaker #2: : I have two siblings now, and that is a good number. My brother is two years younger than me. I also have a sister who is four years younger than me. We all get along well and rarely argue or fight.

c. Speaker #3: If I had the chance to play polo, I think that would be fun. I like horses, so playing a sport on horseback would be cool. Even if I didn't play polo well, I still think it would be fun to try.

Track 27

6 **Listen to each response and match it to the question it answers.**

Response #1: If I had a chance, I would buy a vintage Porsche Spyder. I would buy this car because James Dean always drove around in this car. It is actually the car he died in. I've always loved James Dean. He was so cool, so I would buy the same car that he loved in hopes of one day being a little bit like him.

Response #2: If I got a chance, I would live in a French chateau in the Loire valley. This is known as the valley of the kings. The landscape is beautiful, the castles are incredibly elegant and well preserved. The food and wine is as good as anywhere in the world. This would undoubtedly be where I would choose to live if I had the chance.

Response #3: If I had a chance, I would study Chinese. Chinese is the most commonly spoken language in the world. China is also gaining business might every day. It would be an advantage for my future career if I were able to speak Chinese. I believe Chinese will be the language of the future, so I would choose to learn it.

Unit 10 Inventions and Discoveries

Track 28

① **Listen to the speakers. Check the type of answer the speaker gives.**

a. Speaker #1: Even though the radio doesn't seem very exciting today, I think people will still listen to the radio in the future. Maybe they won't listen to regular radio stations. These days, satellite radio is popular. I think the radio of the future will be free satellite radio for everyone.

b. Speaker #2: I would like to invent a robot that would take care of my dog. If the robot could feed my dog and take it out for walks, that would be great. It would save me a lot of time! It wouldn't need to play with my dog, though. I would still do that.

c. Speaker #3: One example of something that was invented a long time ago but that we still use is the wheel. I used two wheels to come to class today. I rode my bike here. If the wheel weren't invented, we wouldn't have bikes today!

Track 30

⑥ **Listen to each response and match it to the question it answers.**

Response #1: The most dangerous invention in human history is gunpowder. Gunpowder effectively neutralized human strength and fighting skill.

Gunpowder has enabled killing to be done at a distance, and it has also made killing much more efficient.

Response #2: I think our lives would be much better without the invention of TV. Before TV, people had to be creative to keep themselves entertained. Now, people just sit in front of the TV. I think TV has made society lazy and uncreative.

Response #3: The invention of the steam engine was important because it first captured vast amounts of power. The steam engine provided so much more power than animals that factories and giant boats were able to develop. The steam engine helped to transform society.

Unit 11 Money

Track 31

① **Listen to the speakers. Check the type of answer the speaker gives.**

a. Speaker #1: I think it is better to invest in gold rather than in stocks or bonds. Gold is something that you can hold in your hand, and it has real value. Another good reason to invest in gold is because it doesn't lose value as easily as stocks or bonds. It's a safer investment.

b. Speaker #2: Last summer, I worked at a job that paid me minimum wage. I worked in a fast food restaurant for about two months. It wasn't a hard job, and I ended up saving over $1,000 over the summer. I think it was a good experience.

c. Speaker #3: The last thing that I bought for over $10 was a book for one of my classes. I paid for the book using cash. I try not to use a credit card when I buy things. Most of the time, I try to have enough cash with me to buy the things that I need to buy.

Track 33

⑥ **Listen to each response and match it to the question it answers.**

a. **Response #1:** I would always choose the job that gives more satisfaction. People spend more time at work than anything else. You don't want to have to spend eight hours a day every day doing something that you hate, regardless of how good the salary is.

b. **Response #2:** The saying "Show me the money" has two very important meanings. The first meaning has to do with the fact that people need to have an incentive to do something. The second and more important meaning is that talking means very little unless there are actions or some kind of proof behind the talk.

c. **Response #3:** Yes, I got an allowance when I was little. I would receive twenty-five cents every week. I spent half of my money on things that I wanted, and I saved the rest of it. Eventually, after many years, my brothers and I were able to pool our money together to buy a video game system.

Unit 12 Parenting

Track 34

❶ **Listen to the speakers. Check the type of answer the speaker gives.**

a. **Speaker #1:** When I was little, I used to go camping with my father. I was in the boy scouts, so we went camping together several times each year. There were other boys on those camping trips as well, but it was a really good way for me and my father to spend time together. I have lots of good memories from those campouts.

b. **Speaker #2:** My parents didn't reward me for good grades. Some of my friends got money for good grades, but not me. Of course my parents told me that they were proud of my grades, but they didn't want me to just work for good grades so that I would get money.

c. **Speaker #3:** I think it is important for parents to talk to their kids about things like drugs, smoking, and alcohol. If parents don't talk about those things, then kids might think that their parents don't care. By talking about these things, parents can clearly

explain how they feel about drugs or alcohol. They can even talk about their own experiences.

Track 36

❻ **Listen to each response and match it to the question it answers.**

Response #1: Parents can teach their children the values of their culture, traditions, and customs because every family preserves its culture in its own way. This could be anything from religion to facts about the family's history. It is always a good idea to learn lessons from the successes and failures of our ancestors.

Response #2: Parents should do quality activities with their children such as sport and educational games. When parents play sports or games with their children, everyone enjoys time together and children can learn how to play games with the right attitude. They don't always have to win. They just have to enjoy spending time with others.

Response #3: Yes, they should. Parents should require participation in household chores from an early age because children have to learn that they are a part of a family. For example, children should be required to clean their own dishes and make their own beds.

Unit 13 Space Exploration

Track 37

❶ **Listen to the speakers. Check the type of answer the speaker gives.**

a. **Speaker #1:** I don't think a human will walk on Mars during my lifetime. Mars is too far away, so people can't really travel there to explore it. Anyway, I don't think it's practical to try and send people to Mars. Scientists should put more time and effort into studying how we can live here on Earth, not on Mars.

b. **Speaker #2:** I don't think there was a full moon in the sky last night. It was kind of cloudy, so I didn't actually see the moon last night. But I remember that a couple of days ago there was only a crescent moon. It's too soon to have a full moon yet.

c. Speaker #3: The most interesting planet to me is Saturn. That is the planet with rings around it. There aren't any other planets in our solar system with rings. That makes Saturn unique.

Track 39

⑥ **Listen to each response and match it to the question it answers.**

Response #1: No, I don't believe horoscopes are true at all. That is just a way to pass the time and have some fun. In fact, the charts people use today were created a long time ago and might not accurately reflect the positions of the stars today.

Response #2: The first man to go into space was Yuri Gagarin, a Russian cosmonaut, aboard the *Vostok* 1 spaceship on April 12, 1961. He made one orbit around the earth. He became a hero in Russia and worldwide.

Response #3: We know in the past that people used telescopes to count the stars and to observe their positions. Telescopes have been in use for hundreds of years. Before telescopes, people had to look up at the night sky with their naked eyes.

Unit 14   Superstitions

Track 40

① **Listen to the speakers. Check the type of answer the speaker gives.**

a. Speaker #1: I learned about one superstition when I was in elementary school. That superstition had a saying. It went like this: Step on a crack and break your mother's back. So when I was walking home from school each day, I would be careful to try not to step on any cracks in the sidewalk.

b. Speaker #2: In my country, the number four is unlucky. But in the United States, four is not an unlucky number. The first time that I rode an

elevator in the US, I was surprised to see the number four on the elevator buttons. In my country, you never see that. They always just write the letter "F" on that button in my country.

c. Speaker #3: One bad luck superstition is related to walking under a ladder. I think this superstition has some logic to it. If a person walks under a ladder, there is a chance that the ladder may fall or something above the ladder may fall. So it's safer to avoid walking under ladders, which is what this superstition recommends.

Track 42

⑥ **Listen to each response and match it to the question it answers.**

Response #1: Yes, I do. I do believe in this superstition though some people think that I am silly. I don't know why, but every time I see a black cat in the street, I try to move very slowly so that it doesn't cross my path. I have never had bad luck from this, but I will probably never change.

Response #2: : In my country, the number eight is considered very lucky, as is being born on the eighth of the month, or finding eight of anything. This is because the god of luck has eight arms. This means that if you encounter the number eight, in any form, you are going to be blessed with good luck.

Response #3: Yes, they do. We believe in the Chinese horoscope in our culture, and we often check it before we make a major change in our lives, like a big purchase or a wedding. My parents told me that if a horoscope says not to do something, you should wait one year, and have your horoscope checked again.

Unit 15   Television

Track 43

① **Listen to the speakers. Check the type of answer the speaker gives.**

a. Speaker #1: I don't think it is healthy if a person sits too close to a television while they're watching

it. A person should sit at least one meter away from the screen. If you sit too close to a television while watching it, you may damage your eyes.

b. Speaker #2: In our apartment, we have a DVD player and a home theater sound system hooked up to our TV. My dad loves to watch movies, so he bought all that equipment. The DVD player can hold three different discs at the same time, but usually we just put one in at a time.

c. Speaker #3: My family had three televisions in our house when I was growing up. The TV that we used most often was in the living room. That was where we all watched TV together in the evenings. There was also a TV in my parents' bedroom and another small one in our kitchen.

Track 45

⑥ **Listen to each response and match it to the question it answers.**

Response #1: Life would certainly be different without TV. Probably we would be able to occupy ourselves in other ways. We could read books, talk more to other people, and engage in more active pastimes such as sports. If we didn't have TV, we probably wouldn't miss it.

Response #2: People shouldn't spend too much time in front of the TV because it contributes to a sedentary lifestyle, which may cause obesity. People should have a balanced, active lifestyle. This could include time in front of the TV, but should also include exercise so that the person stays healthy.

Response #3: We have cable TV at home. This gives us about one hundred channels. The hardest part is deciding what to watch as there are so many to choose from. My favorite channel is the one that shows cartoons from about twenty years ago. I think they are much funnier than cartoons today.

Track 46

① **Listen to the speakers. Check the type of answer the speaker gives.**

a. Speaker #1: I recently had a lot of stress from a difficult family situation. At that time, I didn't want to talk to my friends or anything. I just wanted to be alone. Luckily, I live near the beach, so when I want to be alone, I just walk along the beach and think. That really helped relieve my stress during that difficult time.

b. Speaker #2: Probably one of the most stressful jobs is being a doctor. In some cases, a doctor has a person's life in their hands. I can't imagine how stressful that would be. Certainly, I have no desire to ever be a doctor. I'd hate to have a job with that much stress. And I don't like the sight of blood either.

c. Speaker #3: Usually when I feel stress, I start sweating and I get a headache. Taking aspirin doesn't help much when I have a stress headache. The only thing that works for me is taking a nap. After I wake up, my headache is usually gone and I don't feel so stressed out.

Track 48

⑥ **Listen to each response and match it to the question it answers.**

Response #1: I like to read in my free time. I like all kinds of books, but most of all, I like science fiction novels. I also like to go walking to help myself relax. I live far from the city, in the mountains, so the air is fresh and walking is very relaxing.

Response #2: I would choose an easy job with low pay because I don't want to get sick from being constantly exposed to stressful situations. No salary is worth being constantly sick from stress. If you were sick and unhappy, it would be more difficult to enjoy the extra money you have.

Response #3: Yes, I do. A problem shared is a problem halved. Trying to deal with stress on your own only makes you feel more stressed. Very often a friend can help you to feel better if you talk to them about your problems. Sometimes they can even do something for you to make your problems go away.

Unit 17 Memories

Track 49

❶ Listen to the speakers. Check the type of answer the speaker gives.

a. **Speaker #1:** A memorable time in my life was when I went on a rafting trip. I took that trip with the Boy Scouts. There were about twenty people on the trip. We went down a river with rapids in big yellow rafts. It was a lot of fun.

b. **Speaker #2:** A good way to develop your memory skills is to practice memorizing stuff. Certain kinds of puzzles are also good for developing the memory. Solving puzzles like crosswords and number puzzles can really help older people keep their brains active, so they won't have memory problems.

c. **Speaker #3:** I broke my arm when I was young, but I don't really remember much about it. I remember wearing a cast on my arm in school. But the actual time and place when I broke my arm is gone from my memory. My mom says I did it on the playground. I just don't remember at all.

Track 51

❻ Listen to each response and match it to the question it answers.

Response #1: I remember one of my elementary school teachers. My favorite one was Mr. Craven. He was so cool. Every Friday he would bring his guitar to school, and if we were good, he would sing in class.

Response #2: My favorite photo is a family photo taken when all of my family was together during the holidays. My brothers and cousins and I were all young. My family's fireplace is in the background, and since it was late, my brothers and I were in our pajamas.

Response #3: The most unpleasant event of my life was when my friend told on me for saying a bad word. I was in first grade. The teacher scolded me for it. I felt embarrassed, but mostly I was angry with my friend who got me into trouble.

Unit 18 Phobias

Track 52

❶ Listen to the speakers. Check the type of answer the speaker gives.

a. **Speaker #1:** I know someone who is afraid of heights. It is my older brother. We went to one of those tall buildings with a restaurant on the top floor. He refused to sit at a table near the window, so we had to sit by the wall.

b. **Speaker #2:** It is natural for children to be afraid of the dark. There is probably some natural instinct in humans to avoid dark places. Dangerous things might be waiting in dark places. Snakes and spiders live in those kinds of places, so our instinct tells us to avoid those places.

c. **Speaker #3:** Some people are really afraid of speaking in front of large groups of people. Maybe everybody feels that way to some extent. Some people are just better at overcoming the fear and standing up there and talking. Others can't overcome that fear.

Track 54

❻ Listen to each response and match it to the question it answers.

Response #1: I think people are afraid of going to the dentist because they associate this place with pain. There are also some pretty scary-looking dentist's tools. I had to have root canal surgery which not only hurt a lot, but it cost me a lot of money.

Response #2: People are afraid of dogs because they think that the dog might bite them. However, most dogs never bite those who treat them kindly. Dogs sometimes bark loudly as you walk by them, but that is only because they are protecting their owners'

properties. I have never had a bad experience with a dog.

Response #3: When I was little, I was afraid of the monster that I thought lived in my closet. When my parents opened the door and it wasn't there, I thought it had just gone away for a minute. I only learned later that it was only the changing shadows that looked like a monster.

Unit 19   Social Issues

Track 55

❶ **Listen to the speakers. Check the type of answer the speaker gives.**

a. Speaker #1: I had some trouble getting medical help once because of the poor state of my country's national health care system. I needed an operation on my knee. The problem was that the hospital was full. I had to wait four months before I could schedule the operation. It was terrible!

b. Speaker #2: My definition of poverty is a level of wealth that is less than $6,000 a year. Why did I choose that number? That amount is equal to earning $500 a month. I think if someone earns less than that amount in this country, he or she is living in poverty.

c. Speaker #3: The best way to get the crime rate of a city under control is to make sure citizens have what they need. If most citizens in a city have a decent job, good medical care, and suitable places to live, then the crime rate will be low. When people don't have these things, the crime rate goes up.

Track 57

❻ **Listen to each response and match it to the question it answers.**

Response #1: Crime rates in my country are reasonably low, except in the capital. In the capital, there is a high rate of unemployment, and this causes many people to turn to drugs. This has also led to a high crime rate since many drug addicts commit crimes to pay for their drugs.

Response #2: My country has one of the best healthcare programs available. If you don't have private healthcare, you can visit any public hospital, and they will immediately take care of you. We also have arrangements with foreign countries, so that if you are injured abroad, you don't have to pay for healthcare.

Response #3: : The most important thing governments can do to keep families from falling below the poverty line is to maintain a high level of education. The more educated someone is, the more likely they are to succeed and get a good job. It is also important to supply accommodation to those who cannot afford it as housing is frequently a major source of expenditure.

Unit 20   Media and News

Track 58

❶ **Listen to the speakers. Check the type of answer the speaker gives.**

a. Speaker #1: I didn't watch the news on TV last night, but I did read the headlines online. I have my favorite news website bookmarked on my computer, so I can check the news there easily. One of the headlines that I read last night was about my country's recent presidential election.

b. Speaker #2: I don't think there is much danger of radio ever disappearing. Plenty of people still enjoy listening to music or talk shows on the radio. Radio stations may need to think of creative ways to get more listeners, but I don't think they have to worry about losing their audiences completely any time soon.

c. Speaker #3: I rarely buy newspapers. I get my news from free sources like television news programs or online news sites. My parents still buy newspapers, though. My mother likes to look through the newspaper to find coupons.

Track 60

❻ **Listen to each response and match it to the question it answers.**

Response #1: Mass media deliver news and information to the majority of any population. They can influence the way we look at events because we are at the mercy of what they are telling us. Most citizens do not have access to the type of information that the mass media have, so people who control media are able to pick and choose which stories the general public gets to hear.

Response #2: News is an event that piques people's interest. This can be anything from war, to finance, to celebrity gossip. News is important because it often affects people's lives. Weather is often one of the most watched segments of the news because the weather affects people's lives, too.

Response #3: The issue that always seems to be in discussion is the Middle East. It always seems as if someone is fighting and dying in the region. The news also seems to highlight links between terrorists in other countries and certain groups based in the Middle East.

Unit 01 Meeting People

① **Listen to the speakers. Check the type of answer the speaker gives.**

a. **Speaker #1:** [ ] personal experience
[X] personal opinion

b. **Speaker #2:** [X] personal experience
[ ] personal opinion

c. **Speaker #3:** [ ] personal experience
[X] personal opinion

② **Sort the phrases by writing them in the correct categories.**

Weekend Activities: visiting a museum, watching a movie, relaxing with friends, going hiking

Bad Events: the death of a loved one, an extended hospital stay, being in an accident, breaking a bone

Life Goals: getting a good education, starting your own company, having children, owning a home

④ **Choose one of the questions below. Prepare your answers to this question by writing notes below. Use the questions from part 3 to help with your notes.**

Answers will vary.

a. **What do you usually do on the weekends?**

On the weekend, I try to do something exciting or different. During the week I work hard and do the same thing every day, so I really try to enjoy my weekends. I like to go hiking, or perhaps visit a museum I haven't been to before.

b. **Describe the unhappiest day of your life.**

The unhappiest day of my life was when I broke my leg. It was a really silly accident! I tripped over the sidewalk in my haste to cross the street to get to an ice cream store. I had to spend all day in hospital, and no one came to see me.

c. **What is your goal in life?**

My goal in life is to get a good education, specifically in science. I want to open my own company to make new medicine to help sick

people. I believe global health is a very important issue, and people need affordable medicine.

⑥ **Listen to each response and match it to the question it answers.**

a. 2

b. 1

c. 3

❖ **Extra Practice**

Try answering one or more of these questions for extra practice. Use at least three sentences in your response to each question.

Sample Responses

1. **Are you an outgoing person? Explain.**

Yes, I am outgoing because I love meeting and being with people. I always look forward to going dancing, going partying, or doing something fun with my friends. Sometimes, when we meet new people, we invite them to my house and have a party.

2. **Describe one thing that can improve your mood instantaneously.**

Chocolate can instantly improve my mood when I am unhappy. I love the taste, but my mom, a pharmacist, explained it has something that produces a chemical called serotonin. This is what makes it addictive.

3. **What inspires you to be creative? Why?**

I like the final result of my creativity; that is why I like to create. For example, when I draw a picture, I always step back and take a long look. I also really enjoy it when my friends look at it and smile. Then I know that they like it.

4. **If you won $1,000,000 in a lottery, how would you spend it? Explain.**

If I won $1,000,000 in a lottery, I would like to invest as much of it as possible because I could live off the interest and dividends. However, I would also give some to charity because it would be nice to improve the quality of life for people who are poor or sick.

Unit 02　Sports

❶ Listen to the speakers. Check the type of answer the speaker gives.

    a. Speaker #1: [X] personal experience
                       [ ] personal opinion

    b. Speaker #2: [ ] personal experience
                       [X] personal opinion

    c. Speaker #3: [X] personal experience
                       [ ] personal opinion

❷ Sort the phrases by writing them in the correct categories.

Sumo Wrestling: traditional sport of Japan, matches are over quickly, is an old sport, played by fat men

Sports Fans: attend many games, collect memorabilia, follow favorite teams, know about players

Drugs in Sports: are illegal, used by some athletes, can enhance performance, give an unfair advantage

❹ Choose one of the questions below. Prepare your answers to this question by writing notes below. Use the questions from part 3 to help with your notes.

Answers will vary.

a. What is a traditional sport of your country? Describe it.

Sumo is a traditional sport of my country. It's an old sport filled with rituals. The aim is get your opponent out of the ring or on the ground. Sumo wrestlers are normally fat, powerful men.

b. Are you a sports fan? What is your favorite team?

No, I'm not a sports fan the way I understand it. To be a real sports fan, you have to attend all the games of your favorite team, know everything about its players, and collect memorabilia of your team. I don't do all that, but I have a favorite team. They are not the best team, but they have the most heart.

c. Do you think athletes should be allowed to take drugs to enhance their performance? Explain.

No, I think taking drugs to enhance performance is immoral. It is also illegal. Using drugs gives an athlete an unfair advantage over other players. Even worse, drugs can have serious negative effects on an athlete's health.

❻ Listen to each response and match it to the question it answers.

    a. 1

    b. 3

    c. 2

❖ Extra Practice

Try answering one or more of these questions for extra practice. Use at least three sentences in your response to each question.

Sample Responses

1. Who is your favorite basketball player?

My favorite basketball player is Michael Jordan. He used to play for the Chicago Bulls. He is probably the greatest basketball player of all time. I have his jersey, his shoes, and a basketball with his autograph on it. He was very exciting to watch. He was so popular that he even has his own breakfast cereal.

2. Do you think hunting and fishing are sports? Explain.

No, I don't. I can't imagine having hunting or fishing as an Olympic sport. There are probably a lot of sports-related lessons you can learn from both, and I am sure you need strength and endurance, but I cannot see killing an animal as something to strive for in competition and as a spectator sport.

3. Why do you think professional athletes change teams frequently?

I think one reason professional athletes change teams frequently is because they are looking for better opportunities to develop their game skills by practicing with various coaches and players. I

think that many athletes sell themselves too. They are paid such extraordinary amounts of money that I don't really blame them. I would probably do the same.

4. Should advertising companies use professional athletes to promote their products? Explain.

I think using professional athletes for advertising is a good idea as long as they aren't advertising anything bad for you, such as cigarettes. People often look up to professional athletes and view them as role models. This means athletes have a certain amount of responsibility towards their fans.

Unit 03 Friendship

1 Listen to the speakers. Check the type of answer the speaker gives.

  a. Speaker #1: [ ] personal experience [X] personal opinion

  b. Speaker #2: [ ] personal experience [X] personal opinion

  c. Speaker #3: [X] personal experience [ ] personal opinion

2 Sort the phrases by writing them in the correct categories.

Attributes of a Best friend: makes you laugh, cares about you, enjoys the same activities, similar interests

Places to Meet: at a party, at school, at church, in a club

Long-Distance Friendships: stay in contact, talk on the phone, talk through email, lots of effort

4 Choose one of the questions below. Prepare your answers to this question by writing notes below. Use the questions from part 3 to help with your notes

Answers will vary.

a. Describe your best friend.

Dan is such a funny and entertaining guy. He always makes me laugh, but at the same time, he really cares about me. He is my best friend because we have so many similar interests. We've been friends ever since we first met each other in elementary school.

b. Where do you think is a good place to meet new friends?

I think the best places to meet friends is in a school club or social club because there you are most likely to meet people with similar interests. It is always easier to become friends with someone with whom you have something in common. Yes, a place where you are comfortable and where you have fun is also a great place to meet new friends.

c. Do you think it is possible to maintain a long-distance friendship?

Of course, it is possible to have a long-distance relationship. With the Internet, it is so easy to stay in contact with people. You can call or email them nearly everyday. As long as both friends are willing to put in the little bit of extra effort to stay in contact, there is no reason why it cannot work.

6 Listen to each response and match it to the question it answers.

a. 3

b. 1

c. 2

❖ Extra Practice

Try answering one or more of these questions for extra practice. Use at least three sentences in your response to each question.

Sample Responses

1. Explain the proverb "A friend in need is a friend indeed."

The proverb "A friend in need is a friend indeed" means that only those friends who are ready to support you and do everything for you in difficult situations are your real friends. Often when people are faced with a difficult situation, they learn who their real friends are by seeing who comes to support and help them when they need it the most.

2. Do you agree with the following saying "Books and friends should be few but good"? Explain.

I think you can have as many friends as you want or need. Some people are great at connecting with others. Certain friends act as support for different people in different ways. I do not agree with the saying. With both books and friends, you need to have as many as you need in order to make sure that you do not miss a great book, or even worse, a great friend.

3. What does the Chinese proverb "Do not remove a fly from your friend's forehead with a hatchet" mean?

The proverb "Do not remove a fly from your friend's forehead with a hatchet" means that if you try to help your friend, make sure you provide the help that your friend needs and can benefit from. If you are a real friend, you will never hurt your friends physically or emotionally. It also means that you must always be mindful of how you help your friends. Doing something to help that will end up hurting your friend is not being a friend at all.

4. Explain the Spanish proverb "It is better to weep with wise men than to laugh with fools."

This means that it is better to spend time with wiser people, even if the circumstances are not that happy, than to spend time with people who don't know much. It means that you should spend time with wiser, more intelligent people and not with shallow people.

Unit 04 **Holidays**

❶ **Listen to the speakers. Check the type of answer the speaker gives.**

a. **Speaker #1:** [X] personal experience
　　　　　　　 [ ] personal opinion

b. **Speaker #2:** [X] personal experience
　　　　　　　 [ ] personal opinion

c. **Speaker #3:** [ ] personal experience
　　　　　　　 [X] personal opinion

❷ **Sort the phrases by writing them in the correct categories.**

A Family Get Together: big feast, everyone comes home, catch up, traditional foods

Valentine's Day: : dinner date, box of chocolates, romantic, roses

Businesses: commercial, promotions, profits, sales

❹ **Choose one of the questions below. Prepare your answers to this question by writing notes below. Use the questions from part 3 to help with your notes**

Answers will vary.

a. **Do people celebrate Thanksgiving in your country/culture?**

Yes, we celebrate Thanksgiving. We always go to our grandparents' house and have a big feast. We enjoy traditional dishes, sit around and catch up with all of our relatives, and see how their lives are going.

b. **Describe how you celebrate Valentine's Day in your country/culture.**

Valentine's day is a huge holiday in my country. You see hearts, chocolate, and roses for sale everywhere. People go out for dinner and exchange gifts, like boxes of chocolates, flowers, and cards. It is supposed to be a really romantic holiday, but I think it's all just a waste of money.

c. **How do businesses make money on holidays?**

Businesses make money through promotion and sales of specialty items specifically designed for the holiday. The big holidays have become too commercialized these days, so they're not really fun anymore. Because they make so much money, businesses have started to promote even minor holidays in hopes of making a profit.

6 Listen to each response and match it to the question it answers.

a. 1

b. 3

c. 2

❖ **Extra Practice**

Try answering one or more of these questions for extra practice. Use at least three sentences in your response to each question.

Sample Responses

1. How do you celebrate birthdays in your family?

Birthdays are not a big deal in my family. Most of us do not really care about them, and we do not like the extra attention paid to us. Normally, we go out to a nice dinner together and then go home at the end of the night. We usually do not receive any extravagant presents or get any more attention than we normally do.

2. Is there a Teacher's Day in your country/culture?

Yes, there is a Teacher's Day in my culture. It is in late spring. We usually honor our teachers by giving them presents and cards that show how much we appreciate their effort in helping to make our lives better.

3. What is your opinion about making New Year's resolutions?

I rarely make New Year's resolutions. In the past I have made them, only to find myself a week into the year breaking that resolution. I have tried to exercise more and study harder, but I have found that I always go back to the way that I was acting before.

4. When do you celebrate a Mother's or Women's Day in your country/culture?

We usually celebrate Mother's Day in my country in May. To celebrate the day, we always call and do nice things for our mothers. We usually take our mom out for a nice dinner or go to brunch. We also buy our mom a nice gift to show how much we appreciate all that she does for us.

Unit 05 **Stereotypes**

1 Listen to the speakers. Check the type of answer the speaker gives.

a. **Speaker #1:** [ ] personal experience
[X] personal opinion

b. **Speaker #2:** [X] personal experience
[ ] personal opinion

c. **Speaker #3:** [X] personal experience
[ ] personal opinion

2 Sort the phrases by writing them in the correct categories.

Stereotypical Women's Roles: faithful wife, caretaker of the house, housekeeper, good cook

Physical Jobs: machine operator, construction worker, mechanic, fisherman

The Stereotypical Man: stronger than women, enjoys physical labor, masculine, swears a lot

4 Choose one of the questions below. Prepare your answers to this question by writing notes below. Use the questions from part 3 to help with your notes.

Answers will vary.

a. **What is the typical woman's role in a family in your culture?**

The typical woman's role in a family in my culture is a faithful wife, caring mother, and good cook. I think women are expected to do all these things because it is what they have traditionally done. It is often seen as the woman's responsibility to be the caretaker of the house.

b. **What are typical jobs/occupations for men in your culture?**

Most jobs that deal with physical labor such as construction typically belong to men. Mechanics and heavy machinery operators tend also to be men. I think that these jobs are typically male jobs because they involve a lot of dirt, sweat, and pain, which are things that are often embraced in a male culture.

c. What language/vocabulary is considered appropriate for a man to use but inappropriate for a woman in your culture?

In my culture, it is OK for men to swear or use strong language. It is not seen as a big deal by most people. Women who swear in public are often labeled as uncouth or unladylike. This is because women have traditionally been seen as pleasant and soft-spoken.

⑥ Listen to each response and match it to the question it answers.

a. 2

b. 1

c. 3

❖ **Extra Practice**

Try answering one or more of these questions for extra practice. Use at least three sentences in your response to each question.

Sample Responses

1. What colors are acceptable for a woman to wear but are unacceptable for a man? Explain.

Although people in my culture have become more tolerant to what men and women can wear lately, I think it would still be a bit surprising to see a man wearing pink or light yellow because it's considered to be a traditionally feminine color. If a man wears pink or yellow, he will often be teased or mocked by his buddies for dressing up like a little girl.

2. Can a woman be a "breadwinner" in your culture? Explain.

More and more, women have started to be known as primary "breadwinners" in society. This is due to various laws and changes in attitudes that have allowed women access and promotion to high-powered jobs in society. In many places women no longer experience a "glass ceiling" on their careers and as a result, they are able to earn more than enough money to be the primary financial contributor in a home.

3. Is it acceptable for a woman or man to show strong emotions in public? Explain.

I don't think that men or women should show their emotions in public. When people become emotional, they often become irrational and make bad decisions. They can also make others around them very uncomfortable. Both sexes should be treated fairly and equally, and thus I think that both sexes should be expected to control their emotions in public.

4. How is a certain body image formed and promoted in society?

I think that the biggest determinant of how someone should look is due to how the rich and powerful look. The body shape that is harder to attain, I think, is the more desirable body shape. Now, everyone wants to be slim, fit, and tanned because it shows that you exercise outdoors. But in the 18th century, food was rare, and everyone had to work outside all day, so plump people with very white skin were considered beautiful.

Unit 06 **Time Management**

① Listen to the speakers. Check the type of answer they speaker gives.

a. **Speaker #1:** [X] personal experience
[ ] personal opinion

b. **Speaker #2:** [X] personal experience
[ ] personal opinion

c. **Speaker #3:** [ ] personal experience
[X] personal opinion

② Sort the phrases by writing them in the correct categories.

Daily Planning: keep track of deadlines, upcoming assignments, important events, appointments

SchoolWork: attending lectures, taking notes, studying, reading

Sleep: during the night, close your eyes, a time for resting, usually in bed

④ **Choose one of the questions below. Prepare your answers to this question by writing notes below. Use the questions from part 3 to help with your notes.**

Answers will vary.

a. Is it important to keep a daily planner, calendar, or a PDA?

Yes, it is. It's very helpful for keeping track of deadlines and upcoming events. I like using a wall calendar because I can make note of important events and see everything that I need to accomplish this month at a glance. If I didn't use a calendar, I would probably forget appointments I had made.

b. How could you minimize the time that you spend doing your homework, studying, and reading?

I could minimize the time I spend doing my homework and studying by paying attention at school and taking notes of my teachers' lectures. When I pay attention at school, I learn much faster and better. I also find it much easier to remember and understand the information we have been taught. When I take good notes in class, I probably spend an hour or two less studying for those classes.

c. How much time do you spend sleeping?

I usually sleep for about 6-7 hours each night. I don't think it's enough because I always have difficulty waking up in the morning and staying awake in my first class. I would love to stay in bed longer, but I just have too much to do each day and not enough time.

⑥ **Listen to each response and match it to the question it answers.**

a. 3

b. 1

c. 2

❖ **Extra Practice**

Try answering one or more of these questions for extra practice. Use at least three sentences in your response to each question.

Sample Responses

1. Give examples of things that make you waste a lot of time.

I think I waste a lot of time on waking up. My mom has to shout to get me out of bed. I also waste a lot of time waiting for the bus. Sometimes it is just late, and sometimes it doesn't show up at all. Public transportation can sometimes be unreliable.

2. Do you procrastinate? Give examples of how and when you procrastinate.

Yes, I procrastinate sometimes. When I was in grade school, I didn't like doing my homework, so I would put it off till the last minute. My mother used to get very angry with me for doing that. Now, I try to start my work early so that I have enough time to finish it. But I still procrastinate when it comes to cleaning my room!

3. If your friend invites you for a birthday party, is it OK to be late? Explain.

Yes, it's OK to be 10-15 minutes late. Actually, it's customary in my culture to be a little late for parties because you give your friends a chance to finish doing their last-minute preparations. It is also a little unfashionable to arrive early. I don't understand why.

4. Explain the saying "The early bird gets the worm."

"The early bird gets the worm" means that if you start doing something early, you have more time to accomplish it, you don't have to be in a hurry, and you will get rewarded for not wasting time. For example, if you start working on your major assignment early, you will finish in time, without being stressed out.

Schooling

① **Listen to the speakers. Check the type of answer the speaker gives.**

a. **Speaker #1:** [ ] personal experience
[X] personal opinion

b. **Speaker #2:** [X] personal experience
[ ] personal opinion

c. **Speaker #3:** [ ] personal experience
[X] personal opinion

② **Sort the phrases by writing them in the correct categories.**

Home Schooling Advantages: study areas you like, fits your own learning style, slower paced learning, flexible schedule

Public School Advantages: develop social skills, communicate with teachers, fit in with peers, access to school facilities

Computer Disadvantages: can hurt your eyes, no face-to-face interaction, carpal tunnel syndrome, harmful for kids

④ **Choose one of the questions below. Prepare your answers to this question by writing notes below. Use the questions from part 3 to help with your notes**

Answers will vary.

a. **What are the advantages of being schooled at home?**

There are many advantages to being schooled at home. For one thing, you can go at a pace that best suits your own learning style. Students can also focus on areas that they are interested in. Another advantage is that homeschooled kids are able to have a more flexible school schedule.

b. **What important skills do children acquire in public schools?**

Besides studying, children also acquire important social skills that help them fit in with their peers. These kinds of skills are important because later in life, kids will have to fit in with co-workers or

people in other groups they belong to. Another advantage of attending public school is that students have access to facilities like the school gym, the school computer lab, and the school performance hall.

c. **Do you think it could be harmful for children to spend a lot of time in front of their computers?**

Yes, spending too much time in front of the computer can be very harmful for children. Constant exposure to computer screens can hurt children's eyes. It can also potentially lead to other disabilities like carpal tunnel syndrome. Children need to learn to interact face-to-face with other people to be functioning adults.

⑥ **Listen to each response and match it to the question it answers.**

a. 3

b. 2

c. 1

❖ **Extra Practice**

Try answering one or more of these questions for extra practice. Use at least three sentences in your response to each question.

Sample Responses

1. **Where do you think children experience more peer pressure: through homeschooling or public schooling?**

Children experience more peer pressure through public schooling, of course, because they are exposed to more kids at school than in their neighborhoods. At school, children can communicate with and be exposed to other children. Homeschooled kids have far fewer opportunities to be exposed to other children. As a result, kids who attend public schools experience far more peer pressure than homeschooled ones.

2. **What can children do when they have difficulty studying or doing homework?**

When children have difficulty with studying

or working, they have many options. They can always talk to their teachers to receive extra help. In addition, there are also programs available through public schools to help struggling students. If a family has enough money, they can also hire a private tutor.

3. **What is your opinion: will more children be schooled at home in the future or not?**

I do not think more children will be homeschooled. I think the number of homeschooled kids will remain fairly constant. Homeschooling requires a lot of effort from the parents that many parents are unable to give due to work and other children. Homeschooled children will also continue to find it difficult to have adequate social lives. This will cause the number of homeschooled kids to remain constant rather than increase.

4. **Describe parent-child interaction when a child starts going to public school.**

When a child goes to public school, parent-child interaction is usually limited to after school and on the weekend. Children are usually off at school during the day, and busy with homework or other activities after school. This leaves much less time for parent-child interaction. However, most parents play an active role in their children's education. They take a great interest in making sure their children do well in school.

Unit 08 Politics

① **Listen to the speakers. Check the type of answer the speaker gives.**

a. **Speaker #1:** [X] personal experience
  [ ] personal opinion

b. **Speaker #2:** [ ] personal experience
  [X] personal opinion

c. **Speaker #3:** [ ] personal experience
  [X] personal opinion

② **Sort the phrases by writing them in the correct categories.**

Governments: monarchies, democracies, dictatorships, republics

Legal Matters: judges, courts, lawyers, appeals

Armies: wear uniforms, do peacekeeping, use weapons, have soldiers

④ **Choose one of the questions below. Prepare your answers to this question by writing notes below. Use the questions from part 3 to help with your notes**

Answers will vary.

a. **Describe various forms of government that exist nowadays and give examples of countries that have these governments.**

Some of the forms of government that exist today are monarchies, democracies, dictatorships, and republics. I find monarchies to be the oldest and the most interesting form of government. Monarchies are interesting because they combine the ancient traditions of royalty with modern forms of government. One well-known example of a country that still has a monarchy is the United Kingdom of Great Britain and Northern Ireland.

b. **What is the highest court in your country, and what kind of decisions does it make?**

The highest court in my country is called the Supreme Court, and it is responsible for ruling on appeals to difficult or controversial legal cases. The Supreme Court deals with all kinds of crimes from murder to discrimination. After the Supreme Court rules on a case, that's it. There isn't any higher court to appeal to.

c. **Why do you think countries need armies?**

Countries need armies because they represent power and ensure national and international security. Army service is not compulsory in my country. Although my country has a small army, it contributes to international security by sending soldiers on peacekeeping missions to several countries, including countries in the Middle East.

6 Listen to each response and match it to the question it answers.

a. 1

b. 3

c. 2

❖ **Extra Practice**

Try answering one or more of these questions for extra practice. Use at least three sentences in your response to each question.

Sample Responses

1. **What is the structure of the government in your country?**

   The government in my country is composed primarily of the Dail. This is made up of over two hundred seats. Each TD—Teach Dail (or minister)—is voted in by the people in his or her area. When an issue comes up, every TD in the Dail votes, and the majority vote wins.

2. **Which branch of the government is responsible for enforcing the laws?**

   The ministry of defense is responsible for enforcing laws. Ultimately, the minister for defense is in charge. However, he delegates the day-to-day policing of the country to the chief of police. National security is controlled by the commandant of the army, including issues such as terrorism.

3. **Who is the chief commander of the army in your country?**

   The chief commander of the army is the Minister for Defense. His duties include command of the police and the army. However, he occupies more of an administrative role, leaving the running of the army and the police to their respective commanders. He is also responsible for maintaining peace between my country and our closest neighbor.

4. **Do people actively participate in elections in your country? Explain.**

   Yes, they do, because people understand that their votes count and their active participation influences

the future of the country. Each constituency has a specific number of seats, and the people with the most votes fill the number of seats available. So if there are four seats available, the four people with the highest number of votes get the seats.

Unit 09 **If You Could**

1 Listen to the speakers. Check the type of answer the speaker gives.

a. **Speaker #1:** [ ] personal experience
   [X] personal opinion

b. **Speaker #2:** [X] personal experience
   [ ] personal opinion

c. **Speaker #3:** [ ] personal experience
   [X] personal opinion

2 Sort the phrases by writing them in the correct categories.

Safari Animals: elephants, hyenas, rhinos, giraffes

A Beach Vacation: go swimming, play volleyball, have a massage, get a sun tan

Movies: on the big screen, sometimes emotional, in a theater, surround sound

4 Choose one of the questions below. Prepare your answers to this question by writing notes below. Use the questions from part 3 to help with your notes.

Answers will vary.

a. **If you got a chance, where would you go on vacation?**

   If I had the chance, I would go to Tanzania for a vacation. I want to go on a safari and see wild elephants, rhinos, and giraffes. I could also see the ancient city of Zanzibar. Tanzania would be the ideal destination for my fantasy vacation.

b. **If you got a chance, where would you be now?**

   If I had a chance, I would be at the beach with my friends now. We would play volleyball, swim, and have fun because I am tired of studying and working hard. Relaxing on the beach while getting a sun tan is just what I need to reduce the stress and anxiety of everyday life.

c. If you got a chance, what movies would you watch again?

If I had the chance, I would like to watch the movie *Life is Beautiful* in a theater. It is a story about a man in a concentration camp during World War II. The movie's theme is to make the best of a situation no matter how grim it is.

6 Listen to each response and match it to the question it answers.

a. 2

b. 1

c. 3

❖ Extra Practice

Try answering one or more of these questions for extra practice. Use at least three sentences in your response to each question.

Sample Responses

1. If you got a chance, what celebrity would you like to meet? Explain.

If I got a chance, I would like to meet Will Ferrell. I think he is the funniest man in Hollywood. I think he always makes really funny movies, and I imagine that in real life he is even funnier. I think that I would be laughing the entire time that I was with him.

2. If you had a chance, what subjects would you study? Why?

If I had the chance, I would study Spanish. In high school, I chose to study Latin because I thought it would help me get a better score on my college entrance exam. I got a good grade, but nobody speaks Latin. It's not useful at all to me now! Spanish, on the other hand, would be really useful for traveling.

3. If you got a chance, what would you change about your life? Explain.

If I had the chance to change my life, I would choose where I was born. When I look around the world, I see so many other countries that have so much more opportunity. My country is really limited. There are few good jobs, and people have to give up everything in their lives to get one of these jobs. This is no way to live, so I would choose to be born in a different country.

4. If you had a chance, what would you have done differently? Explain.

If I had the chance, I would never have eaten the chicken dinner that my friend's mom made. I cannot eat chicken without thinking about the terrible taste of that chicken. I used to love chicken, but now I can't eat it. Had I known what was going to happen I would never have eaten that chicken in the first place.

Unit 10 Inventions and Discoveries

1 Listen to the speakers. Check the type of answer they speaker gives.

a. **Speaker #1:** [ ] personal experience [X] personal opinion

b. **Speaker #2:** [ ] personal experience [X] personal opinion

c. **Speaker #3:** [X] personal experience [ ] personal opinion

2 Sort the phrases by writing them in the correct categories.

Things That Fly: birds, hot air balloons, airplanes, helicopters

Studying Space: cameras, exploration, telescopes, planet watching

Penicillin: fights diseases, helps people recover, destroys infections, fights bacterial infection

4 Choose one of the questions below. Prepare your answers to this question by writing notes below. Use the questions from part 3 to help with your notes.

Answers will vary.

a. What do you know about the invention of flight?

Leonardo da Vinci thought of the helicopter, but he was never able to put this idea into practice. In the early 1900s, the Wright brothers successfully flew the first man-powered machine. Their flight was only a few minutes, but it would soon lead to rapid changes in aviation.

b. What inventions are necessary for space travel?

The most important invention for space travel is an ability to travel quickly over long distances. Space is so vast that unless we can travel quickly, our astronauts will be dead before they reach their destination. The future of space exploration lies on Mars. It is the only planet that is close enough to establish any sort of exploration on. Other than that, we will have to continue exploring space through telescopes and cameras.

c. Describe an important advancement in the field of medicine.

The most important advancement in the field of medicine was penicillin. Penicillin destroys infections allowing a person to recover from injuries without the possibility of a bacterial infection. Without penicillin, all other medical advances in surgery would have been almost impossible, which is why it is the most important.

⑥ **Listen to each response and match it to the question it answers.**

a. 3

b. 2

c. 1

❖ **Extra Practice**

Try answering one or more of these questions for extra practice. Use at least three sentences in your response to each question.

Sample Responses

1. **How and why do people invent something new?**

People often invent something new first by figuring out why they want to invent something, and then figuring out how to invent it. People always have new ideas for why they want to make a new product, but they often don't know how to make it. People want to make new products that can help to change their lives.

2. **Why do you think the invention of the printing press was important?**

The invention of the printing press was important for several reasons. Prior to the printing press, people had to copy every book by hand. This took a long time. The printing press was much faster, and it made many more books available to everyone. This encouraged more and more people to become educated. The printing press made it possible for knowledge to become widely available.

3. **How do you think the invention of computers changed our lives?**

The invention of the computer has made our lives so much easier. Now we have access to so much more information than we ever had in the past. Computers have allowed everyone access to the vast amounts of information available in the world.

4. **Do you think the fields of genetic engineering and cloning have a future? Explain.**

I don't support the idea of genetic engineering and cloning because I think they can bring immense negative effects to humankind if they are misused. People might try to select the kind of children they will have, or they might try to live to an unnaturally old age. In addition, we will have to deal with the rights and responsibilities of those involved in the cloning process.

Unit 11 Money

1 **Listen to the speakers. Check the type of answer they speaker gives.**

a. Speaker #1: [ ] personal experience
[X] personal opinion

b. Speaker #2: [X] personal experience
[ ] personal opinion

c. Speaker #3: [X] personal experience
[ ] personal opinion

2 **Sort the phrases by writing them in the correct categories.**

Investing: property, bonds, stocks, commodities

Gambling: odds, blackjack, poker, bets

Expenses: clothing, taxes, rent, food

4 **Choose one of the questions below. Prepare your answers to this question by writing notes below. Use the questions from part 3 to help with your notes**

Answers will vary.

a. **Do you think it is wiser to save money in the bank or invest it?**

I think it is wiser to invest the money. By investing, money can gain more interest than it would gain from a bank. My father's investments in stocks have taught me this. Extra money should always be invested.

b. **Have you ever gambled?**

Yes, I like to gamble. I have never been to a casino, but I like playing card games with my friends. Sometimes, I play blackjack and poker on weekends at my friend's house. Gambling can be dangerous because some people become obsessed with winning. They may gamble away everything that they have in the hope of winning their money back.

c. **What do you think you spend too much money on (e.g. clothes, shoes, entertainment, video games)?**

I think I spend too much money on food. Every day I buy a couple of drinks, some snacks, and lunch. By the end of the day, I spend ten dollars on stuff that I could have made and eaten at home. I'll probably end up cutting down on the drinks and the snacks, but I'll still go out to lunch every day.

6 **Listen to each response and match it to the question it answers.**

a. 3

b. 1

c. 2

❖ **Extra Practice**

Try answering one or more of these questions for extra practice. Use at least three sentences in your response to each question.

Sample Responses

1. **Explain the saying "Time is money."**

This saying basically means that productive and wealthy people are constantly doing things that make money. Many people with high paying jobs, like lawyers, do not have enough time to meet with all their clients. Wasting their time is in essence costing them money because they could be meeting with clients rather than picking up dry cleaning or going grocery shopping.

2. **Why do businesses often use the "buy now, pay later" approach?**

The "buy now, pay later" approach is great for businesses. First of all, they move their merchandise out of the store. More importantly, they make money off the interest that is charged to the customer.

3. **If you won $1,000,000 in a lottery, what would you do with the money?**

If I won a million dollars, I would quit my job and take my family and friends on a vacation to a tropical paradise. After the vacation, I would take whatever money was left and I would set up a trust fund. I would leave the money in an account, and I would live off of the interest of that money.

4. Where do people keep their money?

Some people hide their money somewhere in their house. This allows convenient access to the money, but if the money is stolen, it cannot be replaced. You can also put your money into a bank. While in the bank, your money earns interest, and it is also very safe.

Unit 12   Parenting

① Listen to the speakers. Check the type of answer the speaker gives.

a. Speaker #1: [X] personal experience
[ ] personal opinion

b. Speaker #2: [X] personal experience
[ ] personal opinion

c. Speaker #3: [ ] personal experience
[X] personal opinion

② Sort the phrases by writing them in the correct categories.

Education: schoolwork, tests, classrooms, homework

Bad Behavior: needs discipline, loses privileges, is unacceptable, deserves grounding

Parents and Children: lots of love, support, encouragement, care

④ Choose one of the questions below. Prepare your answers to this question by writing notes below. Use the questions from part 3 to help with your notes.

Answers will vary.

a. How can parents teach their children the importance of education?

Parents can teach their kids that education is important by setting a personal example and involving themselves in their children's learning. If parents help their children with schoolwork, they show their kids that education is important. This will result in the children taking their

education more seriously and working harder.

b. Do you think parents should discipline their children for misbehavior?

Yes, they should because they have to get the point across that bad behavior is unacceptable and will not be tolerated. However, they shouldn't use physical punishment. Instead, parents should temporarily take away privileges that the children enjoy.

c. Do you think children should support their parents when they get old?

Yes, of course. Children should support their parents when they get old because their parents gave them life, love, support, and care for many years. This is a very common practice in my culture, so there is also some social pressure for children to care for their parents.

⑥ Listen to each response and match it to the question it answers.

a. 2

b. 1

c. 3

❖ Extra Practice

Try answering one or more of these questions for extra practice. Use at least three sentences in your response to each question.

Sample Responses

1. Do you think parents should treat their sons and daughters equally? Explain.

Parents should certainly treat children of both sexes equally. In many countries, it is a legal requirement not to distinguish between people based on their sex. Both boys and girls deserve to be treated as equals and to be given equal rights and privileges in their families and in their societies.

2. When should children start making their own decisions about their lives?

Parents should make this decision based on their good judgment of their children's maturity

because some children are ready to make their own decisions at a very young age; others aren't ready until later on. Making decisions requires knowledge of the possible consequences of their actions, and some children are unable to think things through until they grow older.

3. What do you think grandparents can teach their grandchildren?

Grandparents can teach their grandchildren valuable lessons of life and wisdom. As people age, they become wiser with knowledge that you can't learn at school. Grandparents can teach grandchildren about local history or about life lessons. This is the wisdom that comes from experience, not from books.

4. Recall one valuable lesson that your parents have taught you. Talk about it.

The most important thing my parents taught me is probably respect. This includes not only respect for other people but also respect for their property, their privacy, and their right to have different opinions about things than I do. Everybody deserves to be treated with respect.

Unit 13 Space Exploration

① Listen to the speakers. Check the type of answer the speaker gives.

a. **Speaker #1:** [ ] personal experience
[X] personal opinion

b. **Speaker #2:** [X] personal experience
[ ] personal opinion

c. **Speaker #3:** [ ] personal experience
[X] personal opinion

② Sort the phrases by writing them in the correct categories.

The Sun: provides warmth, gives us light, far away from the Earth, made of hydrogen and helium

Space Exploration: space shuttles, space stations, space suits, space experiments

Telescopes: have lenses, range in size, help us see faraway things, used by astronomers

④ Choose one of the questions below. Prepare your answers to this question by writing notes below. Use the questions from part 3 to help with your notes.

Answers will vary.

a. **What can you explain about the sun?**

The sun is a brightly burning mass of gases. This provides us with the warmth and light that we feel and see from our planet. The sun is mostly made of hydrogen and helium. Light that leaves the sun takes eight minutes to reach the Earth.

b. **What space stations/space shuttles do you know?**

I have heard about the space shuttles that were used by the US for space exploration. Currently, many countries contribute to space exploration, including a joint venture by some countries in Europe. Someday it might be possible for people to live in space, but I don't think that will become reality for a long time.

c. **What is a telescope used for?**

A telescope is a tool with multiple lenses that is used to study stars and other objects in space. Telescopes can range from very small ones to be used at home to very big ones to be used in a space observatory. For really powerful telescopes, you need really big lenses, and that is what limits how powerful a telescope can be.

⑥ Listen to each response and match it to the question it answers.

a. 1

b. 2

c. 3

❖ Extra Practice

Try answering one or more of these questions for extra practice. Use at least three sentences in your response to each question.

Sample Responses

1. **Are horoscopes popular or important in your country? Explain.**

   People who belong to cultures that believe in horoscopes might consult them before they make a major step or a major change in their lives. This is not common where I live. While it is often fun to read the horoscopes in the daily newspaper, it is wiser to use good sense when making important decisions.

2. **What do you know about attempts to explore the moon?**

   There were a lot of attempts to explore the moon. First, people would send rockets to the moon. These rockets would take pictures of its craters and bring back samples of the moon's soil. Then astronauts began to land on the moon. The first man to do it was Neil Armstrong, an American astronaut.

3. **Would you ever consider traveling into space?**

   Yes, I would. It must be pretty exciting to go into space and observe our planet, other planets, and stars from space. I know that space tourism nowadays is only available to the very wealthy. I don't think I will ever have enough money to travel into space since it currently costs millions of dollars.

4. **Do you think there is life on other planets? Explain.**

   Yes, I do. I think there may be life in other galaxies because there are so many of them. However, we will probably never meet aliens. Scientists say you cannot travel faster than the speed of light, and even traveling at the speed of light, it would take a long, long time to get to even the next closest star in our galaxy.

Unit 14 Superstitions

❶ **Listen to the speakers. Check the type of answer the speaker gives.**

a. **Speaker #1:** [X] personal experience
   [ ] personal opinion

b. **Speaker #2:** [X] personal experience
   [ ] personal opinion

c. **Speaker #3:** [ ] personal experience
   [X] personal opinion

❷ **Sort the phrases by writing them in the correct categories.**

What Are Superstitions: faith-based, not based on reason, belief in an unexplained power, not the same in all cultures

Signs of Good Luck: four-leaf clovers, a new penny, spilling salt, a rabbit's foot

Fortune Tellers: are sometimes con artists, predict the future, may have psychic powers, use cards or tea leaves

❹ **Choose one of the questions below. Prepare your answers to this question by writing notes below. Use the questions from part 3 to help with your notes.**

Answers will vary.

a. **What is a superstition?**

   A superstition is a belief in the unexplained power of something or somebody. For example, in a lot of cultures, the number 13 is considered to be unlucky. I am not superstitious at all. I believe superstition is a product of ignorance.

b. **According to some people in your country, what brings good luck?**

   In my country, finding a four-leaf clover, a new penny, or spilling salt can bring you good luck. Some people also carry things like a rabbit's foot for good luck. I have no idea where these ideas came from. These beliefs are really old and have been passed down from generation to generation.

c. **Do you believe in fortune telling?**

   I don't believe in fortune telling. I have never gone to a fortune-teller in my life. In general, I think most fortune tellers are just con artists.

There may be some with real psychic powers, but those real ones are few and far between.

⑥ **Listen to each response and match it to the question it answers.**

a. 2

b. 1

c. 3

❖ **Extra Practice**

Try answering one or more of these questions for extra practice. Use at least three sentences in your response to each question.

Sample Responses

1. Do you have lucky and unlucky numbers of your own? Explain.

No. I believe that anything having to do with numbers is entirely by chance or coincidence. I don't see how a number can be linked to luck and there is no scientific evidence. When I see "lucky" numbers, nothing lucky ever happens to me. The same is true of when I encounter "unlucky numbers."

2. Have you heard of any superstitions related to mirrors?

Yes, I know a superstition related to mirrors. There is one that says if you break a mirror you will have bad luck for several years. I believe it is true. My sister broke a mirror and she was very unhappy for a long time. She broke it five years ago, so hopefully she will be happier in two years.

3. Do you believe in ghosts and spirits? Explain.

No, I don't believe in ghosts and spirits. I think they are just a result of our troubled imagination. Scientists suggest that "bad feelings" that you get when you walk into an old house are actually from noises that are at a frequency too low for you to hear, but can still have a strange effect on your body.

4. A superstition says if your right eye itches, you'll laugh soon. If your left eye itches, you'll

cry soon. **Is there a similar superstition in your culture?**

I have never heard about a superstition like this in my country. My culture is a very serious one, and people make fun of you if you believe in superstitions. Maybe this kind of superstition comes from a place where people have allergies, so their eyes itch a lot.

Unit 15 **Television**

① **Listen to the speakers. Check the type of answer the speaker gives.**

a. **Speaker #1:** [ ] personal experience
[X] personal opinion

b. **Speaker #2:** [X] personal experience
[ ] personal opinion

c. **Speaker #3:** [X] personal experience
[ ] personal opinion

② **Sort the phrases by writing them in the correct categories.**

Types of Televisions: high-definition, plasma, flat-screen, big-screen

Advanced Sound Systems: surround sound, multiple speakers, audio input/output, digital sound technology

Parents' Responsibilities: guide children, explain a show's content, block inappropriate shows, supervise their children

④ **Choose one of the questions below. Prepare your answers to this question by writing notes below. Use the questions from part 3 to help with your notes.**

Answers will vary.

a. **What kind of TV do you have (e.g., HDTV, plasma, flat-screen, big-screen)?**

We have a huge plasma TV. It is over fifty inches wide. The advantages are that everything looks really clear. Movies and programs look much better than on my small television.

b. What sound system do you have with your TV?

We have a home-theater surround sound system that allows us to hear movie-quality sound effects. When I watch a movie, and someone opens a door, it is like a door is being opened right beside me. Our system also has digital sound, so the audio output is really clear.

c. How can parents make sure their children are not watching inappropriate programs?

Parents should supervise and guide their children's TV viewing habits. Parents shouldn't expose their children to shows with adult themes or content. For example, some of the shows during prime time are all about relationship problems. Kids shouldn't watch those kinds of shows.

6 Listen to each response and match it to the question it answers.

a. 3

b. 2

c. 1

❖ **Extra Practice**

Try answering one or more of these questions for extra practice. Use at least three sentences in your response to each question.

Sample Responses

1. Do you think people are becoming lazier because of TV? Explain.

I think there are other things in society that make people lazy. We can't just blame it all on TV. I think people enjoy just relaxing and turning off their brains when they are watching TV. But they need this relaxation time because they probably have to work hard studying or thinking at their jobs all day.

2. Do you think there are too many commercials on TV? Explain.

Yes, I do. I think there are too many commercials on TV because I get a feeling that for every 10

minutes of my favorite program, I watch 10 minutes of commercials. It's so irritating. I don't think it's beneficial to watch so many commercials. All they do is try to promote products I don't really need, so the advertising company can make a profit.

3. Should commercials be prohibited on kids' channels? Why or why not?

Yes, they should. Children are very easily influenced and will want to have everything they see, especially on TV. After watching these commercials, children naturally will want the things advertised, and they will plead with their parents for them. TV regulators should be aware of this, and limit the nature and amount of advertising aimed at selling products to children.

4. Should TV programs be rated? Why or why not?

Yes, they should. TV ratings will give people an idea if programs are suitable for whole-family viewing or if some of them might be inappropriate for young children. I think the government has a responsibility to rate the programs being viewed. If a program has an adult theme, it should definitely not be viewed by young children.

Unit 16 **Stress**

1 Listen to the speakers. Check the type of answer the speaker gives.

a. Speaker #1: [X] personal experience
[ ] personal opinion

b. Speaker #2: [ ] personal experience
[X] personal opinion

c. Speaker #3: [X] personal experience
[ ] personal opinion

2 Sort the phrases by writing them in the correct categories.

Adult Responsibilities: raising children, supporting a family, paying bills, saving for the future

Insomnia: can't sleep, bad for your health, can't relax, can be caused by stress

Time Management: not procrastinating, using time wisely, working efficiently, meeting deadlines

④ **Choose one of the questions below. Prepare your answers to this question by writing notes below. Use the questions from part 3 to help with your notes.**

Answers will vary.

a. What do you think are the main causes of stress?

The main cause of stress is the buildup of responsibility as people get older. When you are young, you are not responsible for anything. As you get older, you have to work hard to earn money. Then you have children and you have to look after them. This all contributes to stress.

b. Why do you think some people have insomnia when they are under stress?

When people are under stress, they can't sleep because they can't unwind and stop thinking about their problems. When you keep worrying about a problem, your mind can't relax. If your brain isn't relaxed, your body can't relax, and you can't fall asleep.

c. How can proper time management reduce stress?

Proper time management can reduce stress by keeping too many burdens from weighing on a person's mind. People who have demanding jobs with constant deadlines can become stressed by others asking if a job is finished or not. Working efficiently allows you to meet your deadlines, and this reduces stress.

⑥ **Listen to each response and match it to the question it answers.**

a. 3

b. 1

c. 2

❖ **Extra Practice**

Try answering one or more of these questions for extra practice. Use at least three sentences in your response to each question.

Sample Responses

1. **How do you deal with school-related stress?**

Coping with school-related stress isn't easy. There are always deadlines for papers and projects, and keeping up my grades is very important. I guess the only real release I have from the stress of schoolwork is playing video games. When I play a video game, I can forget about everything and just focus on the game.

2. **Why do you think some people gain weight when they are under stress?**

One of the reactions of your body to stress can be a feeling of constant hunger, so you start eating a lot, and you can't control yourself. Eating releases chemicals into your body that make you feel good. The more stressed you feel, the more you eat because you want your body to release those chemicals.

3. **Describe a stressful situation that you have been in.**

Once I was procrastinating and wasn't working on my final assignment for one of my classes, but my final grade depended on it a lot. When I finally started on it, it was the day it was due to be submitted. I worked for hours and hours but had left it too late. I handed in a half finished report and knew I would get a poor grade.

4. **How can setting realistic goals reduce stress? Explain.**

If you set difficult-to-reach goals, you work harder in order to reach them. When you fail, even when working extra hard, it increases your stress levels by giving you a sense of failure. By setting attainable goals and reaching those targets, you give yourself a sense of achievement. This makes you feel good about yourself.

Unit 17   Memories

① Listen to the speakers. Check the type of answer the speaker gives.

    a. Speaker #1: [X] personal experience
                      [ ] personal opinion

    b. Speaker #2: [ ] personal experience
                      [X] personal opinion

    c. Speaker #3: [X] personal experience
                      [ ] personal opinion

② Sort the phrases by writing them in the correct categories.

Best Friends: are buddies, know each other, talk closely, play together

Learning: book exercises, practice tests, lessons, assignments

Halloween: receive candy, scary decorations, trick-or-treating, dress up

④ Choose one of the questions below. Prepare your answers to this question by writing notes below. Use the questions from part 3 to help with your notes.

Answers will vary.

    a. Do you remember your best friend from childhood?

    I remember my childhood friend, Valerie, very well. We became buddies when we sat next to each other in class in elementary school. We used to play together in her front yard and talked together for hours.

    b. Do you remember how you began studying English?

    My older sister started learning English long before me. She taught me my first words in English. I remember wanting to be like her so badly that I would sit next to her when she would do her English homework. Eventually, when I started learning English, it was much easier for me because I had been studying with my sister for all that time.

    c. What was your favorite holiday when you were a child?

    When I was little, we used to celebrate Halloween. My mom would always decorate the house with all kinds of decorations. On Halloween night, we would go out trick-or-treating with my dad.

⑥ Listen to each response and match it to the question it answers.

    a. 3

    b. 1

    c. 2

❖ Extra Practice

Try answering one or more of these questions for extra practice. Use at least three sentences in your response to each question.

Sample Responses

1. Describe something you remember about one of your grandparents.

    My grandfather was a really smart man, and I always loved going over to his house. I was always so happy to see him. When I walked into the living room, he was always reading the newspaper. He loved to smoke his pipe, and it was always filled with a cherry flavored tobacco.

2. What do you remember about yourself as a teenager?

    I am so embarrassed now when I think about how I acted as a teenager. I was such a troublemaker. I never listened to my mom and often thought of ways to make my mom's life more difficult. I used to do such a bad job at washing the dishes that my mom would have to redo them later. I was a terror, and now, I feel really badly about it.

3. How well can you recall people's faces and/or names?

    I am quite good at remembering faces but have a terrible time trying to remember a person's name. I can often tell a person where and how we met, but I am awful at remembering what their names

are. Sometimes, if I see a name written down, I have an easier time remembering it.

4. Talk about one thing you would like to forget.

I would love to forget my first boyfriend. I was 18, and I had a really handsome boyfriend. I really liked him at the time, and I thought that he really liked me. But after a month, he broke up with me in order to go out with a different girl. I felt horrible, and even to this day, it still hurts a little bit.

Unit 18 Phobias

❶ Listen to the speakers. Check the type of answer the speaker gives.

   a. Speaker #1: [X] personal experience
                   [ ] personal opinion

   b. Speaker #2: [ ] personal experience
                   [X] personal opinion

   c. Speaker #3: [ ] personal experience
                   [X] personal opinion

❷ Sort the phrases by writing them in the correct categories.

   Different Emotions: afraid, nervous, scared, calm

   Extreme Sports: bungee jumping, skateboarding, parachuting, bicycle racing

   Creepy Creatures: spiders, fish, sharks, snakes

❹ Choose one of the questions below. Prepare your answers to this question by writing notes below. Use the questions from part 3 to help with your notes.

Answers will vary.

   a. Is there anything that makes you nervous or afraid?

I am afraid of spiders. This is called arachnophobia. Unfortunately in my country, there are many large and sometimes poisonous spiders. Often they come into my house, and I see them crawling on the floor or on the ceiling.

   b. Would you consider participating in extreme sports?

Sure, I would. I have done a solo parachute jump from 1000 meters. I have also gone bungee jumping four times. I love the adrenalin rush you get from these sports.

   c. What dangers do you face when you go swimming in the ocean?

When a person goes swimming in the ocean, there are certain marine creatures that live there that might attack a swimmer. For example, I watched a movie about a great white shark that attacked lots of people in the water. I was afraid of swimming in the ocean for a while after I saw that movie, but now I'm not afraid anymore.

❻ Listen to each response and match it to the question it answers.

   a. 1

   b. 2

   c. 3

❖ Extra Practice

Try answering one or more of these questions for extra practice. Use at least three sentences in your response to each question.

Sample Responses

1. Do you like watching scary movies? Explain.

No, I don't. I think those movies are made for people who like being scared, but I'm not one of them. I don't like it when the evil guy jumps out from behind the curtains because it makes me jump too. I try to avoid these movies.

2. Do you celebrate Halloween or a similar holiday in your country? Explain.

Yes, we do. When I was very young, we used to dress up for Halloween. I was a big fan of cartoons, so every year I would dress up as a cartoon mouse or duck. We would walk from door to door, and people would give us sweets or fruit.

3. **Give examples of phobias that you know.**

Phobias are unexplainable fears of something. I know about a few of these fears. Claustrophobia is the fear of enclosed spaces, agoraphobia is the fear of open spaces, and pyrophobia is the fear of fire. I don't have any of these phobias, but I am afraid of large cats. I don't know what that fear is called.

4. **How do you think people overcome their fears?**

People overcome their fears by exposing themselves to them and making themselves do what they are afraid of doing. For example, if you have arachnophobia, you can try touching a small spider. You will quickly see it is harmless, and you will lose a little of your fear.

Unit 19 Social Issues

① **Listen to the speakers. Check the type of answer the speaker gives.**

a. **Speaker #1:** [X] personal experience
[ ] personal opinion

b. **Speaker #2:** [ ] personal experience
[X] personal opinion

c. **Speaker #3:** [ ] personal experience
[X] personal opinion

② **Sort the phrases by writing them in the correct categories.**

Social Problems: poverty, crime rates, unemployment rates, homelessness

Lower Income Families: have a poorer quality of life, can't always buy food, can't afford medication, find it hard to pay rent

Government Programs: daycare facilities, subsidized housing, public schooling, national healthcare

④ **Choose one of the questions below. Prepare your answers to this question by writing notes below. Use the questions from part 3 to help with your notes.**

Answers will vary.

a. **Describe common problems that any society has to deal with.**

Every society has to deal with poverty, unemployment, crime rates, and looking after the homeless. Poverty should be society's first concern because it includes, and can lead to, all the others. Poverty can lead to homelessness if a family can't pay rent or can't find a place to live.

b. **What difficulties do families with very low incomes have to face in their everyday life?**

Families with very low incomes have to face the problems of feeding and clothing their children, paying rent, and getting basic necessities on a daily basis. Low-income families typically have a poorer quality of life. For example, they may only be able to afford low-quality foods which can affect the health of children and adults.

c. **What government programs do you have in your country to help disadvantaged families with young children?**

Government programs include subsidized housing and national healthcare. In my country, the government also provides daycare facilities for families who cannot afford private daycare. I have also seen centers for older children, to educate them further after school and keep them off the streets.

⑥ **Listen to each response and match it to the question it answers.**

a. 3

b. 2

c. 1

❖ **Extra Practice**

Try answering one or more of these questions for extra practice. Use at least three sentences in your response to each question.

Sample Responses

1. What needs to be done to take care of homeless children?

Homeless children should immediately be placed in a caring orphanage. Great care should be taken to place these children with an appropriate new family as soon as possible. A family environment is more beneficial to a homeless child than an orphanage. It is also very important to keep homeless brothers and sisters together.

2. What do you think of medical insurance options in your country?

I think we have good medical insurance options in my country. Medical insurance is very expensive, however, and can consume a large portion of one's salary. My family uses a comprehensive plan, covering any possible injury. Other plans may be cheaper, but they don't cover all possible accidents, and as medical care is so expensive, we don't want to take the risk.

3. What is the level of unemployment in your country?

Unemployment in my country is very low. Most people have excellent jobs because we have such a large export industry. Those people without jobs are sent to reeducation centers where they can learn a new trade or job. Soon after finishing their education, they are given jobs by the major industrial centers.

4. Describe any problems with drugs and drug trafficking in your country.

Drug trafficking is a major problem in my country because many farmers farm the coca leaf. This is used to make cocaine which is exported in vast quantities every year. Foreign governments have banned cocaine and try to force our weak government to give in to their demands about our foreign policy.

Unit 20 Media and News

❶ **Listen to the speakers. Check the type of answer the speaker gives.**

   a. **Speaker #1:** [X] personal experience
                      [ ] personal opinion

   b. **Speaker #2:** [ ] personal experience
                      [X] personal opinion

   c. **Speaker #3:** [X] personal experience
                      [ ] personal opinion

❷ **Sort the phrases by writing them in the correct categories.**

   Parts of a Newspaper: front page, business section, sports section, entertainment section

   How Businesses Use Mass Media: radio spots, Internet campaigns, magazine ads, TV commercials
   Paparazzi: follow celebrities, want hot news, spy with cameras, don't respect privacy

❹ **Choose one of the questions below. Prepare your answers to this question by writing notes below. Use the questions from part 3 to help with your notes.**

   Answers will vary.

   a. **What sections of a newspaper do you read the most?**

   I like to read the front-page articles of every section in the newspaper. Newspapers put the most important stories on the front. By reading the front pages, I get a great idea of what is happening without having to devote a lot of time to reading the whole paper.

   b. **How do newspapers and magazines help with business?**

   Newspapers and magazines can print advertisements and reviews that can help attract customers. Newspapers are read every day by millions of people. Popular magazines also have lots of readers. If businesses want to announce plans or just tell people that they exist, they can use newspapers or magazines to gain exposure that would be difficult to get otherwise.

c. What do you think about how paparazzi get news?

I think that the ways in which paparazzi sometimes get news are really immoral. They spy with their cameras outside of celebrities' houses and clubs trying to get a "sensational" shot that would get them a big paycheck. They should respect the boundaries of people's personal and professional lives.

⑥ Listen to each response and match it to the question it answers.

a. 1

b. 2

c. 3

❖ **Extra Practice**

Try answering one or more of these questions for extra practice. Use at least three sentences in your response to each question.

Sample Responses

1. What kinds of news do you like to watch on TV?

My favorite kind of news to watch is sports news. I love listening to commentaries about my favorite teams. Even though sports are not so important in day-to-day life, I love knowing what is happening with my favorite teams.

2. What are the most popular newspapers in your country?

The most popular newspapers in my country are *The New York Times* and *The Wall Street Journal*. *The New York Times* is one of the most respected newspapers in the country. It tends to focus on many topics that have to do with everything from local to international news. *The Wall Street Journal* is the most trusted business newspaper in the world.

3. How is listening to news on the radio important for our everyday lives?

Listening to the news on the radio can simplify our lives in many ways. The traffic reports are by far the most helpful. They get us to work in a quicker and much more efficient manner. Weather updates are also helpful as they can help us to arrange our schedules accordingly.

4. What is "yellow press" and why is it popular?

"Yellow press" is the term used to describe cheap newspapers and magazines that are especially famous and popular because they present scandalous facts and gossip about celebrities' private lives. They often talk about celebrities and whom they are dating. I think they are popular because people inherently love gossip. We love to know what is happening to others even if it is not really our business.